ME AND

MEMOIRS OF *

DOREEN HAYWARD

Fable Publications

Fable Publications
2 Haines Close,
Aylesbury,
Bucks. HP19 3TS

© Doreen Hayward 2000

Doreen Hayward asserts the moral right to
be identified as the author of this work.

A catalogue record of this book is
available from the British Library.

ISBN 0 9538551-0-4

DP resources provided by Paul Ridgley.

All rights reserved. No part of this publication may be reproduced,
stored in a retrieval system, or transmitted, in any form or by any means,
electronic, mechanical, photocopying, recording or otherwise, without the
prior permission of the publishers.

Printed by *Manuscript ReSearch Printing*
P.O. Box 33, Bicester, Oxon, OX26 4ZZ, U.K.
Tel: 01869 323447/322552   Fax: 01869 324096

ME AND MY SHADOWS

Memoirs of a Guide Dog Owner

CONTENTS

ACKNOWLEDGEMENTS	vii
INTRODUCTION	ix
EARLY DAYS	1
BIDDY	18
HOME WITH BIDDY	35
LASSIE TAKES OVER	47
MY LADY AIRLIE	64
TOGETHER WITH MERRY	86
FABLE	105

ACKNOWLEDGEMENTS

My grateful thanks go to my very special friend Bob Burrows who has been so helpful to me in preparing the manuscript and for his help in countless other ways. Thanks also to Rob Casey who undertook some of the publicity research, and for his friendship. I also thank the Guide Dog Association for allowing me to include some of their photographs. Grateful thanks also go to Paul and Kate Brookes who sent photographs of Fable and Carlo at Teignmouth taken while we were on holiday. I am grateful to Paul Ridgley for inserting the photographs and preparing the book for printing. Finally, I would like to thank all those hard working puppy walkers, especially Jean and Bob Jones for photographs and for their care of Fable while I was away.

Doreen Hayward

INTRODUCTION

My first introduction to the world of Guide Dogs for the Blind came as a result of my wife seeing an article in our local paper. A local Labrador had given birth to eleven puppies, which made quite a story with an eye-catching photograph. The pups were destined for the Centre at Leamington Spa. Then right at the end of the article, it mentioned the fact that puppy walkers were in short supply locally.

My wife had been telling me for months, that Freddy, our ten month old Cairn Terrier, loved other dogs especially when he visited the park, and desperately needed a playmate.

We found out that we came under the Wokingham Centre for puppy walking and, after a phone call to offer our services, we eagerly awaited a visit from a supervisor to be assessed to see if we were suitable. Allie duly arrived and during the next two hours we were to discover that having a Guide Dog puppy was going to be very different from having another family pet. A strict walking and toileting regime was to be the norm. Dried food only to eat and weighed out to the ounce, and definitely no titbits between meals.

Despite these rules, two days later we learnt that my wife had been accepted as a potential puppy walker for the Guide Dog Association but we would have to wait until Freddy was one year old. It wasn't long in coming and one day we had a phone call to say that William, a six week old yellow Labrador Retriever Cross would be arriving the following Tuesday. Were we ready?

Thus began our discovery of a way of life unknown to us before. Under the guidance of Allie, making first fortnightly and then monthly visits, we coped with a need to produce a well-trained puppy. One that would only eat from his bowl when we blew a whistle (and didn't he get worried when we mislaid it), come to heal immediately when being called on a free run, walk in a straight line at the right distance in front without pulling, ignore cats, birds and other dogs, never foul the pavement when out walking and only relieve himself on command in a set place on concrete at home.

On the other hand, we could and did go everywhere with him.

INTRODUCTION

Doors opened as if by magic. William soon became a great favourite in our local supermarket. We took him on trains and buses, to church and local restaurants, which was a good excuse to increase our visits to local pubs to sample a few pub lunches. Fred had a friend to play with and William grew. He grew very big and handsome and very adorable.

"Won't you miss him when he's gone," our friends asked, "Yes," we said, "but we know he has a special job to do. We know we are going to lose him so we just have to accept it." The day came at last when we had to say goodbye. Off he went with Allie, tail wagging and without a backward glance to start the next stage of his training.

INTRODUCTION

It was then a case of waiting to see how he got on. Would he settle? Would he like the kennels? Would he miss us? We heard through the grapevine that he was doing fine, then after three months we had a formal report to say that he was doing really well. It was just like getting a school report for one of our children. That's my boy!

Finally, we heard that he had past all the training with flying colours becoming known by the instructors as Mr. Perfect. When we had a letter and a photograph of William wearing his harness with his new owner who clearly thought the world of him, we were so proud, and knew it had all been worthwhile. Beginners luck, we congratulated ourselves, but by this time we were well into training our next pup. So that is what it is like for us.

Dogs have been regarded as man's best friend since time immemorial until the 20th century when it was recognised that they had the ability to do so much more for people. For most of us a dog is a family pet. To someone like Doreen, a Guide Dog is like a key that unlocks the door and allows her to venture out into the wide world.

This book is not intended to be the definitive history of the Guide Dog Association. No. This story gives an insight into just how one person, on the receiving end of all the countless hours of training Guide Dogs and fund raising, has lived with a succession of animals who have enabled her to do those things that all of us with good sight take for granted. It is a human story, full of dogs and plenty of humour. Once started, I couldn't put it down. So now read on and discover what it is like to have to rely on the finished results of all those hours of hard training that go to produce a working Guide Dog, and also a companion.

Bob Jones
Assistant Puppy Walker

CHAPTER 1

EARLY DAYS

My earliest encounter with a Guide Dog must have been when I was about ten years old and attending a school for the blind where I was educated. The dog belonged to a teacher who had only recently joined the school and who was also totally blind. The teacher taught the infants so I did not know her very well but the fact that she had a Guide Dog fascinated me.

Every morning all the girls were made to line up on each side of a long corridor so that the teacher on duty could inspect us before breakfast. Just before the bell was due to sound, Sweep and her mistress would walk confidently down the middle of the corridor between the two rows of girls. Even at that early age I had developed a love of animals so the sight of that handsome creature and her mistress made a deep impression on me.

I remember clearly that Sweep was golden honey coloured. She looked so big and fluffy I was always tempted to put my hand out and pat her as she went past. At that time I knew nothing about the various dog breeds but I later found out that Sweep was a Golden Retriever, a breed much favoured by the Guide Dog Association because of the temperament.

On the odd occasions when I met Sweep with her mistress as she went about the school I would politely say " good morning Miss," and then I would ask "can I stroke Sweep?" She would explain patiently that this was not allowed, but then she would add kindly, "If you meet us when Sweep is not wearing her harness, then you can pat her." Whenever she was stopped in this way by any of the children she would tell us seriously that we must not distract Sweep when she was working so I never had an opportunity to get to know her very well.

As I grew up I was to learn much more about these dogs and the marvellous qualities they possessed. One of the older girls had an uncle who had a Guide Dog, and I used to ask her to tell me stories about it. I listened with interest when she told me that a Doctor working in Germany in 1916 first realised the possibilities of training dogs to guide blind men. He left a German Shepherd to look after one of his patients in the garden of his clinic while he went away to see to something else. When he came back he was so impressed with the way the dog appeared to be looking after the man, that he got in touch with Mrs Dorothy Harrison-Eustis, an American lady who had established a training school in Switzerland, which was called "L'OEIL QUI VOIT" (THE SEEING EYE). Mrs. Eustis was the first person ever to draw up a proper programme for the training of Guide Dogs.

I was to learn about Captain Liakhoff (pictured opposite) who came to this country as an apprentice trainer in 1933 and did much to establish Guide Dog training in Britain. He was not the first trainer to arrive however; Mrs. Eustis sent two trainers over from her school in Switzerland in 1931, before Captain Liakhoff arrived on the scene two years later. He was sent to replace Mr. Debetaz who had returned to Switzerland unexpectedly.

EARLY DAYS

During the war the Guide Dog Association was having a difficult time. The organisation was still in its infancy and suffering from a shortage of funds in common with many other charities of the day. There was a war on so there was no accommodation for kennels, and no trainers available as every able bodied man was needed for the war effort, apart from the fact that meat was strictly rationed. I may have vaguely heard about these wonderful dogs but I knew very little about them then.

Guide Dogs came to Britain in the late twenties. Captain Liakhoff joined the Association in 1931. Although the Association was very small in those early days, Captain Liakhoff developed many of the training practices still used today. Since the thirties, it has grown out of all proportion. From the humble beginnings of one small centre in Leamington, the association now has seven training centres to its credit.

I have the fondest memories of our pet dog whose name was Major and was always ready for a game with my foster brother and myself. Major was quite small so it came as a surprise to learn that Guide Dogs had to be a certain size and were therefore the larger breeds such as German Shepherds or Labradors and Collies, all larger breeds than little Major who was only a mongrel.

The infant teacher did not stay long at the school. Maybe it was the isolation of the place situated as it was in the very heart of the countryside in Buckinghamshire. We were often cut off from the nearest village and town by snowfalls in winter and it was not unusual for pupils to suffer quite badly from chilblains due to severe cold weather. Wartime shortages meant that the electricity supply was often cut off for hours thus adding to the general bleakness of the building. In summer, we were surrounded by peaceful rolling countryside and it was difficult to believe that men and women were fighting for their lives and for our freedom in Europe while we enjoyed the beauty of England in the summertime.

When I look back I realise that I have known many animals during my life but the ones that will remain the most precious are the dogs that have made such a difference to my life. To date, there have been four who have been my constant companions each one serving me faithfully for ten years at a stretch. I have been proud of every one of them. When I was still at school, I vividly remember making myself a promise, "One day," I said to myself, "I am going to have a dog just like

Sweep." I told my closest friends that as soon as I was old enough, I would have a Guide Dog and it would be just like Sweep. "You can't choose one, you have to have what they give you," my friends would tell me.

In the early days of the association, attitudes to Guide Dogs were not very favourable. I found this very difficult to understand because as far as I was concerned, a dog could only be an asset. I could hardly be expected to realise so early in my development that there were any disadvantages in owning a Guide Dog. I was later to discover that not everyone shared my enthusiastic opinion of dogs, no matter how well trained they may have been. Although it was to be some years before I actually achieved my ambition to become the proud possessor of a Guide Dog, it wasn't until I was twenty-seven, that I was able to enrol for training at the Exeter training centre.

Once you become a Guide Dog owner, sooner or later you have to face the fact that a dog's life span is much shorter than ours. As one grows older, your best companion seems to reach retirement age in an alarmingly short space of time. One day you wake up to the realisation that ten years have slipped by without notice and soon you will once again be on your way to the training centre to start the process all over again with a new dog. This is the time all guide dog owners' dread. The owner faces a number of choices. Of course, the final decision will depend on an individual's circumstances. In many cases, where there is a couple, the partner would probably take over the old dog, but where a single person is involved, choices are limited. I could keep her with me, but I could not manage two dogs. I could ask the association to find her a new home, but that would mean that I would lose touch with her. Alternatively,

I could find a home nearby so that I could visit her occasionally.

Even so, the change over is very stressful to dog and owner. For the owner, it means starting all over again building up a relationship and mutual trust. Teaching the new dog all the various shops and places you have been used to visiting regularly with no bother. The dogs learn very quickly, but inevitably, there are teething problems.

Now I am a Pensioner and waiting to change dogs once again, I look to the future and wonder what the next one will be like. Will she be like Biddy, my first black Labrador, or Lassie, another black Labrador, or will she be like Airlie, a yellow Labrador the same as Merry.

Whatever the colour, it will not make any difference to me because I am totally blind, but one thing is certain, every one of my dogs have had different personalities. Biddy was always particularly protective of me. Lassie, was insecure and rather nervous. Airlie, thought she was a person and not a dog. Merry, always behaved like a mischievous naughty child.

The Association do things differently these days. At one time you just went to the training centre when they had a suitable dog ready for you. Nowadays, you are given an opportunity to meet and handle the dog before you start training with it. You then have a chance to find out if you are going to get along with your new companion.

Not all blind people choose to have a Guide Dog, but over the years the use of a dog as a mobility aid has become more popular among the blind fraternity. Due to increased traffic conditions, it is much easier to rely on a dog's eyes, rather than use a long cane, which can be extremely hard on the nervous system. These days teaching methods have changed, and visually impaired children are taught mobility while they are still at school. In my schooldays, the only mobility aid available was a white stick which I disliked intensely, but while I was still at school, I was never formerly taught to use it, you were simply expected to get on as best you could on your own. It wasn't until I left school and finished training as a telephonist that I was ever forced into using a white stick.

I was born in Luton during the thirties. My arrival must have been a disappointment to my parents who wanted a boy. It must also have been a nasty shock to them when it was realised that I was blind. As far as could be traced it was not hereditary. The Doctor told my parents that I had a condition known as Glaucoma, which was usually found in old people. It was caused by pressure in the eye and he suggested they should take me to Moorfields Eye Hospital where they might be able to help. I underwent one or two operations, which gave me back a little sight but not enough for an ordinary education.

Like other parents faced with similar problems they took the advice of the welfare services of the day and sent me to a Sunshine home for blind children at the age of five. Parents were not encouraged to visit in those days and I remained there for two years without being allowed home. My parents were advised that if I were to return home for a holiday, or if they visited too often, this would unsettle me. It would be much better for me in the long run, they said, if they just left me to them for the time being.

I think my parents thought that I would be kept in this type of home permanently but this was not to be the case. Sunshine homes, as they were known, took in babies, some of whom had been abandoned, as well as children at the normal age of five for starting school, and prepared them for life in the bigger schools. At the age of seven, children were dispersed and sent on to continue their education elsewhere. The Sunshine homes were in fact infant schools although they catered for a number of very small children as well as babies.

I was originally sent to a school in London in 1939 but was quickly evacuated at the outbreak of war. My new school was a large country mansion in Buckinghamshire where it was believed the children would be safe from enemy bombing.

I received an elementary education but at least we were taught Braille. Music played a large part in my education. Indeed, I was taught piano and I shall always be grateful for the pleasure music has brought me. We were certainly encouraged to do as much for ourselves as possible. No backsliding in this respect was tolerated, as discipline was rigid. We were however allowed home for school holidays. Most of the children were from London and would return to school with the most horrendous stories about the air raids being made on London.

It was not easy to make friends during my short school holidays although I made friends with neighbouring children. My mother fostered a young boy of my own age and I was never excluded from any of the activities he got himself involved in. He obviously knew all the neighbourhood children otherwise things might have been much more difficult and lonely for me than they otherwise were. Life at home and life at school were two different worlds. I had my friends at school, but I really didn't have any friends of my own at home.

My parents were not very wealthy. My father was a factory worker and my mother worked in catering. We lived in a two up and two down house with what we called a scullery and outside toilet built onto the back. The family consisted of five - my parents, my older sister Joan, myself when I was at home and of course Ron, the little boy my parents fostered. We lived in the kind of neighbourhood where everyone knew each other. Most of our playmates went to the same school apart from myself and Ron, who attended a private school. Holidays were the happiest time of my childhood where I enjoyed a measure of freedom denied me at school. My father owned two allotments that he cultivated, and which Ron and I visited with my father practically everyday to collect fresh vegetables and to feed the rabbits, which he kept. He also looked after an old cart horse and some pigs which he used to feed, and on these occasions he would often lift us on to old Ned's back so that we could ride him out to graze. My mother worked in the catering trade and my father grew all his own vegetables, plus the fact that we kept rabbits for the pot, we didn't suffer from rationing as much as we might have done. Wherever we went we were always accompanied by Major, our dog, who would scamper to and fro, joining in any game we happened to be involved in at the time. Major wasn't our only pet. We also had a cat and a few chickens, apart from the rabbits. As my father had spent his youth in the country, he was well used to caring for animals. There wasn't the amount of traffic on the roads in those days so we were pretty safe but Ron was always put in charge and told to look after me.

We were a pretty close knit family. Aunts and uncles came to visit frequently and as my grandparents lived quite near, we visited them practically every day. My grandmother took in lodgers so the house was always humming with activity. My grandfather played the clarinet and on Sunday nights all the lodgers would join the family for a singsong around the piano with grandfather playing his clarinet. Those were indeed happy occasions as everybody joined in the fun. Sometimes, these Sunday evening gatherings would take place at a friend's house. Wherever they took place, they were always enjoyed by all.

When the holidays finished I would be heartbroken at having to return to school where there were no home comforts and where I missed my parents and all the things that made life worth living.

Life at school was very institutionalised. You were expected to follow the rules and turn up on time wherever you were supposed to be at any particular time. We did things to bells. There was a bell to get up in the morning, one to tell you to line up for breakfast, another to tell you to line up for school, and so on through the day. The food left a lot to be desired and to this day I cannot eat porridge which was always badly cooked, usually burned and lumpy when served with monotonous regularity at breakfast time. As we lined up in the mornings ready for inspection, the smell of frying bacon would waft along the corridor. We were inevitably disappointed as soon as we reached the dining room to find that the bacon was destined for the staff and not for the pupils.

You had to be tough to grow up at Dorton House, school for the blind. Some of the staff could be extremely harsh when it came to handing out punishments. It was not unusual for physical chastisement to be meted out to any unfortunate child who happened to offend. The fact that we were disabled did not make any difference to the treatment handed down to those reckless enough to fall foul of authority. Such abuse would not be tolerated today. Fortunately, teachers and caring staff are much more aware of children's needs these days.

Visiting was restricted to once a month for girls and once a month for boys alternately. It was not always possible for parents to visit because of the school's location tucked away as it was in the heart of the countryside. Travel was also difficult during the war when petrol was rationed and timetables were constantly being interrupted, plus the fact that in my case my parents could only manage to visit perhaps once in each term.

Each week we were expected to write a duty letter home. This would be written in Braille, and the teacher would then write in print underneath, so parents could read what had been written. My father took the trouble to learn a bit of Braille, just enough to be able to write to me. I was always so proud when I received one of the letters he wrote. My mother used to tell me that it took him hours to put a letter together because he had never had a lot of schooling in his younger days. When we received mail from home, it was given to us in the recreation room where the teacher would then read private letters out loud where everyone in the room could hear what was being said. There was no such thing as privacy. We ate together, we slept in dormitories together and we did our lessons together. Whenever I received one of dad's letters I would creep away quietly to devour the precious contents in private where nobody would know what was in it unless I chose to tell them. Happily, things got easier when the war finished and new staff started arriving at the school.

However, my schooldays were not quite all gloom and doom. I gained many friends and indeed I am still in touch with one or two, who were special. I was taught to read and write Braille as soon as I arrived at the school. I often wonder what life would be like without the ability to use Braille so I have to be grateful to those who gave me the skill.

We were never allowed out on our own until we were at least fourteen or fifteen years old. By that time, I suppose it was judged to be safe. Victorian attitudes still persisted among the staff however and girls and boys were not allowed to spend time together except in lessons and in the dining room. As with most rules, ways were quickly found around these restrictions, but if anyone was unfortunate enough to be caught out of bounds they could expect a heavy punishment. Without a doubt, they could even run the risk of expulsion.

Red letter day was *"going home day"*, and was the last day of term. The whole school would hum with excitement. After an early breakfast, everyone would gather with their cases ready to walk down to the little halt, which served the village. There was a two-carriage train that ran between High Wycombe and Bicester three times a day and was known as the Coffee Pot. We were so isolated that this was the only public transport for the locals apart from a couple of busses, which ran on market days from a nearby village.

As the entire school congregated on the up line side of the platform, waiting for the Coffee Pot, there would be a buzz of excitement. As the distant smoke was sighted, and the chug of the little engine got louder, as it gradually began slowing and steaming into the halt, a cheer would go up from all the children who then crowded into the carriages. Some of the boys would engage the engine driver in conversation questioning him about the engine and the railway. Even the children who didn't live in London or the surrounding districts and would be going in different directions used to join the crocodile of children walking down to Dorton Halt on that particular day.

I longed to be away from the restrictions of boarding school. I used to dream about being ordinary and attending a day school like all the children I knew at home. As I grew older and began to think about what I would do when I eventually left school, it was presumed by my parents and the staff at Dorton that I would stay on for an extra four years and train on the knitting machine. This was about the only training available to girls who did not particularly shine in the field of academic achievement. The school ran training courses on two types of knitting machines and most girls went straight onto one or other of them as soon as they were sixteen. The boys fared better as they had the choice of piano tuning, shoe repairs, or basket making, all good trades. Those who were fortunate enough to have a gift for music, or who showed academic abilities above the average were sent on to other colleges or training centres.

I was determined that I would not continue on at Dorton after the age of sixteen. Not only would I be kept there for a further four years suffering all the restrictions of the place, but on completion of training I would then be sent to London to work in workshops for the blind, and have to live in a hostel.

This was not going to happen to me. I made up my mind to train as a telephonist. I heard on the grapevine that the training was only three months and then you were free to return to your home and find work. Despite the opposition from the principal at Dorton who did his utmost to persuade my parents to allow me to stay on at school, I was adamant and finally got my own way after making several threats to abscond if I was forced to return.

After much argument I managed to shake the dust of Dorton House off and start living what I considered to be a normal life. Things had changed at home during the previous year. My foster brother had gone to a boarding school, and my elder sister who had recently married now had a home of her own. This meant that I was the only one left, which made me feel unexpectedly lonely since all the playmates Ron and I used to know had also grown up and were now starting jobs of their own. I thought life was going to be comparatively plain sailing when I eventually finished my training and came home permanently. Finding work did not come easy but I finally found a job on a switchboard.

I quickly settled down to a routine of work but as I worked in a big department store in the centre of town, my mother insisted that I carry a white stick. She pointed out that it would make other people aware of the fact that I was blind. I took great exception to being labelled as different and started playing a little game of my own.

As I walked down our road I would drop the hated article over a neighbour's front garden wall when I thought no one was watching. I used to leave it on buses or in shops. If I could find somewhere convenient to drop it without being noticed, I would. Invariably, it would be discovered. As I endeavoured to put as much distance between me and it, someone would rush up and say "You've left this behind dear!" and return the wretched thing to me. Neighbours would find the stick in their gardens and return it to my mother. She quickly saw through my deception and would severely scold me when I arrived home minus my white stick.

Slowly, I became reconciled to the white stick but suggested to my mother that I should apply for a Guide Dog. Unfortunately, the association had an age limit, which was twenty-one. At that time dogs were in very short supply and young people in their teens were not being considered for training. "I am afraid you will have to wait until you are older," my mother told me, and as little Major was still with us but growing old she added reflectively, "perhaps it would make Major jealous to have another dog in the house after so long on his own." Major was still providing me with companionship and so I agreed to let the matter rest for the time being.

It was to take a further ten years before I was actually able to apply again for a dog. During those ten years I met and married a man who befriended me in the early days when I first started work. We used to go dancing, an activity I enjoyed enormously. We also bought a tandem and went cycling. We drifted into marriage in 1951 and quickly settled down to married life. My first son was born in 1952. I was not expected to work after my marriage but I always intended to go back as soon as I could.

I was to have three little boys quite close together so my life was taken up with being a housewife and mother. That particular period of my life was extremely busy. I had to learn a great deal and it took a lot of adjusting to my new circumstances. Caring for three small children was a fulltime job and left me no time to think about Guide Dogs.

When Major finally joined his companions in the sky at the age of fifteen, my father replaced him by giving me an old English Sheep Dog. He turned out to be a very faithful old friend who refused to be parted from me. If I got on a bus without shutting him up before I left, he would chase after it.

On several occasions I was embarrassed when the conductor stopped the bus and allowed Monty to jump aboard saying "Come on boy, you deserve a ride after running like that." On another occasion, Monty decided to accompany me to hospital and jumped into the ambulance with me. Fortunately, I was only being picked up for an appointment and after a little coaxing, we managed between the driver and myself to persuade Monty to stay at home. There was one awful occasion when Monty had to be forcibly dragged from under the bed. I was in labour and nobody had noticed that he had sneaked into the room and gone undercover. He used to guard my little boys so well that no one dare touch them when they fell and needed to be picked up. The neighbours always came and told me because Monty never allowed anyone to touch them when they were playing.

It was really Monty who decided me to try again to apply to the Guide Dog Association. Although he was not nearly as well trained or behaved as a Guide Dog, he used to guide me enough to enable me to avoid obstacles especially when I had a pusher to manoeuvre. I thought that if an ordinary pet could do that much, I might as well have the real thing.

Some time elapsed before I knew that my application had been accepted. Guide Dogs were becoming more and more popular among the blind. When I finally received a reply to my application, I was informed by the training centre that there was a long waiting list, but I would be called as soon as there was a suitable dog available for me. At last, the long awaited letter arrived offering me a place on the next class, which was due to take place at Exeter and would begin in June 1959. I hastily made arrangements to leave home and family in the capable hands of my mother for a month while I was away training.

By 1951 the value of dogs as a mobility aid had been realised among visually impaired people. The demand had increased so much that the Association had opened its second training centre in Exeter. We all thought it was such a shame that I could not train at the nearest centre which was the bigger one in Leamington Spa. Exeter was a long way from home and I would have to travel there on my own.

Before I could leave, however, there was one more important arrangement to make. It was not possible for us to keep two dogs and we decided that Monty would have to be re-homed. It was a sad day when we said goodbye to our faithful friend and I hoped that he would be as happy in his new home as he had been with us.

CHAPTER TWO

BIDDY

As I climbed out of the trainer's car the old familiar feeling of home sickness crept over me. All I could hear was the twittering of birds and nothing else. For one awful moment memories of boarding school came flooding back! I had expected to be greeted by a chorus of barking dogs, after all, this was a Guide Dog centre, but where were they? The trainer had told me that his name was Mr. Mills, and that he would be training me. As I waited for him to collect my belongings from the boot of his car, I could gladly have turned tail and headed back to the station to catch the next train home. Desperately, I thought of my three children left behind in Luton and wondered guiltily why I had ever wanted a Guide Dog.

"Where are the dogs," I asked uncertainly, "I can't hear any." "Wait until feeding time," he replied cheerfully, "You'll hear them all right then. We have to be careful of noise otherwise we get complaints from the neighbourhood" he told me. "The kennels are all round the back of the building, that's why you can't hear them from the front." Picking up my bag he said "Come on, take my arm and I will show you up to your room."

Carefully, he guided me through the entrance hall and up the stairs giving me a running commentary on where we were going as we progressed, and explaining that I would be sharing with another young lady about my own age. As we reached the bedroom door and went in he said, "later, when all the students have arrived, we will be giving you a conducted tour of the building so that you can become thoroughly familiar with the surroundings".

Before leaving me to unpack and tidy myself up after the long journey from Luton, he quickly showed me round my room making sure I knew where things were. Then, giving me directions on how to reach the lounge, he suggested that I should join the rest of the students downstairs as soon as I was ready.

Following the sound of voices and the chink of teacups half an hour later, I was able to locate the lounge easily. Mr. Mills was there and also the other instructor whose name was Mr. Evans. Mr. Mills quickly introduced me to the other students and to Mr. Evans who was busily handing out cups of tea. There were to be six of us altogether but one student had not yet arrived. The class would consist of three gentlemen and three ladies plus the two trainers so we were evenly matched. Mr. Mills told us that the course would start officially after the evening meal when we would be getting an introductory talk. In order to break the ice and get to know each other, the two trainers assigned to the class would be taking us out afterwards to a local pub for a drink.

I sat down next to my room mate slipping comfortably into conversation with her. We were both in our twenties and would probably find we had a lot in common. The trainer had already made the introductions, so we chatted happily as we exchanged information about ourselves, and I sipped a welcome cup of tea.

My companion turned out to be Welsh and her name was Muriel Wheeler. Unlike myself, Muriel hadn't been married very long so she was quite interested in what I had to tell her about my three little boys aged seven, five and three respectively. She told me that she hadn't been blind very long. Her blindness was caused by an accident when she had fallen downstairs and bumped her head. This had resulted in split retinas, which were not repairable. From the way she spoke, I gathered that Muriel was having tremendous trouble adjusting to her new condition. I explained that I had always been blind and that if she would allow it, I would do my best to help her.

Muriel had been lucky. The neighbours had not been slow in offering the young couple help. They had felt so concerned for her that they had collected enough money between them and donated it so that she could have a guide dog.

It was not uncommon in the fifties for people to donate a certain amount of money so that a dog could be trained. This practice had to be dropped in later years because of the danger of interference with a working unit. It was felt that this could easily occur, if a person or a group of people had provided the finance for a particular individual. The Association therefore made it a rule that all money donated in this way had to go into a common pot to be used for the benefit of all instead of allowing the usual stipulation of where and how the donation should be spent.

In my case no such collection had been made on my behalf. We were not exactly well off with three children to bring up. I had been hard put to finance myself away from home for a month, which was the length of time needed for a blind person to train, and in addition, find enough money to offer for the dog. When trained, the Association asked that each person would give as much as they could easily afford towards their dog but it was not compulsory, you still got the dog even if you couldn't afford to give anything. This rule was later changed again as the Association's finances grew. Nowadays, all Guide Dog owners are only required to pay 50 pence for their dog. That way, everybody can afford a dog but it was not the case in those early days.

As soon as the evening meal was over, Mr. Evans, who was the senior instructor gave us the promised talk which included the house rules and a brief word about the training we would be receiving. He welcomed us to Cleve House and said he hoped we would enjoy our stay. "Make yourselves at home," he said, "there are tea and coffee facilities in the little kitchenette just outside the door to the students lounge and you can make one whenever you like." Then, he went on, "Those of you who have been to boarding school might feel that you are back in an institution when I tell you that you will not be allowed out unaccompanied. We want you to get used to walking with your dog while you are here. We will be taking you out so there is no need to feel that you are back at school. When you have your dogs you will find that there is plenty to do. For the next two days you will be given basic training on the handle before you get your dogs on Sunday."

Cleve House had once been a country residence and was bought by the Association in 1951 as it expanded and needed larger premises. The house was converted into the second training centre with accommodation for ten students and kennelling for about a hundred dogs. After the talk we were shown the layout of the particular section of the house we would be using. First, we went upstairs to the bedrooms, which were on the first floor and all fitted out with basins and provided with dog beds. We were told that we would be expected to keep the dogs off the furniture. Downstairs we were shown the dining room and the entrance hall. Just outside the door of the student's lounge there was a passage, which led down a few steps to a basement area and an exit door. A short path led to the grooming room and kennels where we would have to feed and groom our dogs. This was particularly interesting to me because I had heard that these kennels were supposed to be among the most modern in the country and had under floor heating for the dogs when the weather was cold in winter. Indeed, the dogs were so quiet that I had begun to wonder where they were being kept but Mr. Evans told us that the main kennel block was a little further away from the kennels, which were used for the class dogs. We were then taken to the paddock where we would be able to free run our dogs. The rest of the evening was spent happily socialising in the local pub where we enjoyed a drink before returning to the centre and retiring for the night.

On Saturday morning we began our training in earnest. Promptly at nine o'clock we all gathered in the student's lounge ready to start work on the handle. The instructors explained that we would each be taken out into the grounds individually but at this stage of the training they would be acting as the dog. "If we used a real dog it would get bored very quickly because this part of the training involves a lot of stopping and starting," Mr. Mills told us.

I was chosen to go first and I followed Mr. Mills out onto the drive where he showed me the harness and explained that the front bit fitted round the dog's breast and across its shoulders. There were two rings on each side where the handle of the harness was clipped on. Then he showed me the correct starting position and how to gesture with my forearm and give the command "forward" at the same time. Mr. Mills was holding the front part of the harness at doggy height as I held the handle. As soon as I gestured and gave the command "forward", we seemed to take off. We were walking much faster than my normal pace with a white stick, but as soon as I said, "sit", we stopped dead. We practised this a few times and then learned how to turn right and left. I felt good as I returned to the student's lounge to make way for Muriel. I thought that working with a Guide Dog was going to beat trying to get around with a white stick.

One by one we were taken out into the grounds of Cleve House and put through our paces. In my ignorance, I thought I knew a thing or two about dogs and getting about, but I was to find out that pet dogs were a very different thing to a trained dog. When I was first interviewed by a trainer there were many questions to answer. Questions such as my height, personal preference for breed, family circumstances and environment etc. The trainer still had to assess whether he had matched the right dog to the individual he was training

At the end of the first day's training, Muriel and I took stock and compared notes as we got ready for the evening meal. We had learned a great deal but Muriel wasn't feeling very confident. She obviously thought that she would never manage the training but I told her that things would be different as soon as we got the dogs. We were to receive them on the next day after lunch and we were all looking forward to meeting our canine companions for the first time. There was quite a ritual attached to this event it seemed. All the students would be sent to their rooms and given a plate of titbits. The dogs would then be delivered to the various rooms so that the student could start getting acquainted with the aid of a plate of titbits. Naturally, we were all looking forward to the moment when we would meet our new Guide Dogs, after all, this was what it was all about. There was a general air of expectancy as we met in the student's lounge after lunch the next day. First of all, the special equipment was given out. This consisted of the harness, brush and comb, and a shammy leather. Then the list of dogs allocated to each student was read out. We were then sent to our rooms to await the new arrivals.

Muriel and I sat on our beds holding the plates of titbits and straining our ears to hear the first approach of the trainers coming up the stairs with the dogs. I wondered anxiously if my dog was going to like me. What would I do if it didn't? I comforted myself with the thought that if things didn't work out at least I had tried.

We were both to have black Labradors. My dog was called Biddy, and Muriel's dog was Beauty. I shall never forget the feeling of excitement as Mr. Mills opened the door and the two Labradors came bounding in. He put one leash in my hand and the other one in Muriel's warning us both not to allow the dogs to get too boisterous, he left us alone to make friends with our future Guide Dogs.

What lovely creatures they were too! As I reached down to stroke Biddy's head I thought how soft and smooth her coat felt, it reminded me so much of velvet. When she came into the room I was sitting on the bed. The first thing she did was to knock me backwards as she jumped for the plate of meat and biscuits sending the whole lot flying in all directions. I don't think Beauty was quite as fast as Biddy but there was a general scuffle as they both dived after the spilt treats which we were supposed to have given them in small bits. We laughed as we retrieved the leashes and tried to control the excited animals. We were to be allowed half an hour with our newly acquired friends and then we were instructed to report back to the lounge with our dogs to go through the house drill, which would take up the rest of the afternoon.

Biddy and Beauty were identical black Labradors. We were lucky because they had both been puppy-walked. This scheme was only started in 1955 when Guide Dogs began their own breeding programme.

As soon as the puppies were old enough to leave their mother, they would be taken to one of the many dedicated individuals who volunteered to look after them for approximately twelve months. During this time the puppy-walker would house train them and teach them to walk properly on a lead. They would also socialise them by taking them into various situations they might encounter in later life while working as a Guide Dog. The puppy would also be taught a certain amount of obedience before being returned to the centre to start being trained as a Guide Dog. All this time the puppy would be monitored and when the supervisor considered it ready, it would be taken back to the centre to start its training.

It is not surprising that these generous volunteers often get very attached to the puppies they look after for so long. When this time comes, the Association replaces the first puppy with a new one to start the whole process over again.

In order to keep records straight, as each litter was born all the puppies were given names beginning with the same letter of the alphabet. We hadn't been told officially but as we sat in our bedroom admiring our dogs, we thought that they were probably from the same litter although Muriel seemed to think that all black Labradors looked the same.

There was a definite light hearted atmosphere in the student's lounge that evening as we gathered to discuss the various qualities and characteristics of our charges. Apart from the two black Labradors, there was a Border Collie, a Boxer and two German Shepherds. They were all beautiful dogs and extremely well behaved - at least we thought they were. We were soon to discover that we had a pickpocket in our midst as things began to mysteriously disappear from our pockets. Someone suddenly missed a packet of cigarettes. Then a bunch of keys went missing. Next to disappear was a packet of sweets. A certain amount of scrabbling around on the floor revealed chewed up paper and the remains of the cigarette packet. Amid a great deal of laughter, the culprit was discovered to be a Border Collie called Tessa belonging to Dulcey Marshal, the other lady on the course. Tessa became quite well known for the expertise she achieved with this trick, which often created a laugh, but sometimes created havoc.

Biddy's favourite trick was to hold my sleeve and show me to a chair. This became very useful later during the years I spent with her. She would often take my sleeve gently in her mouth and lead me to a cupboard where she knew the biscuit tin was kept. I was soon to learn just how intelligent Biddy was, but our first evening together had to be devoted to getting to know each other a little before the real work of guiding could begin.

Poor Muriel was often consumed with embarrassment during the time we spent at Exeter. Beauty had a passion for carrying things. Muriel would often arrive in the dining room with Beauty only to be told that she had a sock in her mouth, or some other article she had picked up. One morning, Beauty arrived down for breakfast carrying a pair of knickers. We all had a jolly good laugh but after that Muriel and I made sure that the drawers where we kept our clothes were always kept tightly shut. I suggested that Muriel should perhaps look to see if Beauty was carrying anything, before she left the bedroom to go downstairs.

The next day training started in earnest. First of all, a gentle walk in the grounds, with me holding the harness and Mr. Mills holding the leash, walking on the other side of the dog. Each student was taken out individually until the dogs got used to us. Training started every morning at nine o'clock when we would all get into the training bus and head for the streets of Exeter where we would put into practice all the various turns and special commands we had been taught when we first started our training on the handle. For the first few days the trainer walks along with the dog and student but gradually, he drops back until finally he is on the other side of the road but still in view. As the training progresses, he drops back more and more out of sight. Of course, he is never far away in case of trouble but as far as possible he tries to keep his distance so that the dog is not distracted. The idea is that the dog takes orders from the student and not the trainer but this is a gradual process.

Gradually, as student and dog begin to establish working relationships, the trainer transfers to a vehicle. This enables him to keep an eye on more than one student at a time, and also it gives the opportunity to practice traffic awareness, something which is very important, if you are to stay alive very long. I speak from personal experience when I say that it takes courage to put your trust in a dog when a car is coming straight at you. This is all part of the training however, but takes some getting used to.

Twice daily we would climb into the training bus to be taken into Exeter for a training session. As we became more confident, we would be given a route and told to come back to where the bus was parked as soon as we had completed the exercise. This needed careful concentration because if you forgot how many roads you had crossed or if you took a wrong turning you could easily get lost. Sometimes, we were told to make our own way back to the Centre and given the route. This was usually done at the end of a day and we would be instructed to meet in the dining room for our evening meal. If anyone failed to turn up, a search party would be sent out to find the missing student.

On one occasion it was I who got lost. I must have taken a wrong turning somewhere but to this day I don't know how I managed to make such a mistake. I was reduced to asking directions from passers by in order to find my way back. When I eventually turned up at the centre very late, Mr. Mills was quite annoyed and told me in no uncertain terms that I should learn to listen in future because he didn't want to have to leave his tea to come looking for lost students.

When we were not out training, we spent our time grooming our dogs and practising obedience with them in the paddock. If two or three of us were in the paddock together, the dogs would often have a high old time playing with each other instead of doing their obedience. Apart from grooming, feeding and obedience training, we attended one or two lectures on animal care. These talks were very useful and interesting, they made me aware of just how much I still needed to learn about dogs although we had always kept a family pet.

Our trainers went off duty in the evenings and we were left to do as we pleased. We would gather in the student's lounge where there was a piano and a radio. Two of the students were very good musicians and would often entertain us. At other times we would just sit and talk or discuss the events of the day. Sometimes, the trainers would take those who wanted to go out for a drink.

My thoughts often strayed to home where I wondered if my little boys were missing me, and if my mother was coping. I had particularly asked that my training should take place in term time so that the children were kept occupied for the most part and to make it easier for my mother who was caring for them while my husband was busy working. Whenever possible he would telephone me to fill me in with all the latest news of the children and what was happening at his end. For my part, I would tell him all about Biddy and how I was getting on with the training although I don't think he had much idea of what I was talking about. We were enjoying a glorious summer in Devon but not even this fact really compensated for the enforced separation. It was not easy to be away from home for four weeks. This was the best way of ensuring that all the time and money that had been put into training the dog thus far, would lead to a successful unit at the end of the period spent with the new blind owner. I consoled myself with the thought that a month out of my life was a small price to pay for the independence I would eventually gain in the next few years.

As time slipped by the training intensified to include many of the situations we might encounter in our daily life.

We went for country walks where there were no pavements and no kerbs to indicate road crossings. As it was midsummer, darkness did not fall until approximately ten p.m. so we only had a brief experience of working with a Guide Dog at night. Since it was so late, this was carried out in the grounds of Cleve House. We went for bus rides and visited the railway station. I found this exercise particularly hair raising. We were required to walk right up to the very edge of the platform and then give the command "forward". Obviously, if the dog actually went forward, we would both fall onto the line. I was

relieved to find that when I gave the command, Biddy passed in front of me to the right and started walking along the platform. As Mr. Mills instructed us he said jovially that if the dog made any attempt to go forward when the command was given, we should just let go of the handle and let the dog fall over the edge. Fortunately, no such accident occurred and after completing the exercise, I beat a hasty retreat to the cafe to enjoy a cup of tea while I tried to restore my shattered nerves.

Previous experience of being guided round an obstacle or obstruction in the road usually left me feeling ruffled. In some cases I would feel quite angry. The kind of thing that often happened would be a member of the public approaching me with an offer to help because there was something in my way. They would then grip my arm firmly, or grasp my elbow or shoulder and simply propel me in front of them round the obstacle where I would be left high and dry. I have spoken to other blind people who have had similar experiences, so now I always make sure that if anyone offers to help me, I get hold of their arm first. That way, they can't just leave me stranded and unsure of my immediate surroundings. People often presume that you want to go across a road, and without asking, forcibly escort you to the other side. This has happened to me on several occasions, and I know it has happened to others.

Because of my experiences I felt a little nervous about going through the obstacle course. This was an artificial collection of sticks, planks, strings, ladders, food on the ground and things that overhang, etc. It was arranged in the grounds of Cleve House for the benefit of the students who were required to walk through it with the dog without allowing anything to touch the right shoulder or allowing any distraction while going through the course. Although we had all managed pretty successfully to avoid the obstacles which were often purposely placed in the way during our walks in the town, the obstacle course was a bit different. Any false move once in it could lead to disaster, like something falling on you. At the very least, it would probably make a noise as it fell and unnerve the dog. Nothing heavy was used so nobody ever got hurt; it just made the dog more careful.

As it happened, I don't think any of us came to grief and I for one breathed a sigh of relief having successfully negotiated the obstacles.

My confidence was shattered once again when it came to traffic training. This took place in the town with two trainers driving cars. My first experience of traffic training left me shaking but in no danger. It seemed that every time I left the pavement and attempted to cross the road, a car would come zooming up to me and skid to a halt in front of me. Biddy would stop dead in her tracks and the car would continue on. This was all part of the training but it was a very nerve wracking part until I got used to it and learned to trust Biddy, who never put a paw wrong. Cars would often back out of driveways as we walked along or a bicycle would come whizzing past the unsuspecting student as we made our way back to the training van. All this kept us on our toes and would often lead to Biddy anticipating the car as we prepared to cross a road. It would then be up to the student to encourage the dog to leave the kerb, so another lesson could be learnt.

Even so, the dogs had a mind of their own at times. I suppose when they thought they knew the new owner well enough, they would try it on. This happened to me with Biddy. One day as I made my way back to the training van I was suddenly hailed from behind. I had gone straight passed the van and the trainer called to me to come back and do the approach once again. I did as I was told and the same thing happened. I had to repeat the exercise four times before Biddy gave up and stopped ready to climb aboard.

Muriel and I often compared notes as we sat in our bedroom in the evenings. As the time progressed, we became very good friends. When I first met her she was very shy and uncertain of herself. By the time we reached the end of our training, she was becoming much more confident. A Guide Dog was going to make a lot of difference to her, but it was also going to make a difference to me. We were both proud of our dogs and longed to show them off to our families. Although I had always managed pretty well with a white stick, I felt conspicuous and self-conscious. Now I was beginning to feel much more confident in myself, and in my ability to get from A to B without having to creep along hugging a wall, and trying to give the impression of not hurrying anywhere in particular.

Our final day at Exeter was spent doing a special walk that would qualify us as Guide Dog owners. After completing this route, we would then be taken individually to the controller of training's office where we would be required to sign a special agreement. We would be asked not to exhibit, or show the dogs, as they were of pedigree stock and could easily be used in the show ring. As it happened, we were informed by the controller that all papers relating to pedigrees had been destroyed so that the dogs could not be used in that way. Breeding was not allowed. The Association did not spay the bitches in those days before they left the centre, a fact that one day I would have cause to bitterly regret. We would have to promise not to allow ourselves to be photographed unless given express permission from the Association to do so.

The next day was rather like school holidays, with everyone going off with their suit cases. We all said our goodbyes and wished each other luck. I was to share the journey to London with one of the other students and I had arranged with my husband to meet the train when we got into Paddington. The Association had reserved a compartment for us so that the dogs would be able to travel in comfort without the danger of being stepped on.

The dogs behaved beautifully on the journey and when we finally arrived at Paddington and alighted from the train, I said goodbye to my companion and hoped we would be able to keep in touch.

I was quickly hurried off by my husband to catch a taxi, that would take us to St. Pancras where we would board another train to complete our journey home.

CHAPTER THREE

HOME WITH BIDDY

Biddy was the immediate success I knew she would be with the children. Peter, aged seven, and Ricky, aged five, begged to be allowed to take her out for a walk and show her off to their friends the minute they saw her. I had a lot of explaining to do as I tried to make them understand that she was a very special dog and would have to be treated with the utmost care.

We lived in a prefab on a council estate where it was not unusual for dogs to be let out in the morning and allowed to run lose in the streets all day until the owners returned in the evening. My little boys thought that they would be allowed to treat Biddy as just another playmate, so it was necessary to firmly lay down a few ground rules right from the outset, and start as I meant to go on. I had learnt a great deal during my training, and I was determined to make sure that my children also understood that Guide Dogs were working dogs. I patiently explained that Biddy could not be allowed out free, and why they should never attempt to give her titbits or feed her with the odd sweet. It was now my turn to put into practice all the things I had learnt while I was training.

Feeling rather nervous, I ventured out the following day to introduce Biddy to her new surroundings. We had a short walk to the local shops where I was greeted with some interest. Neighbours stopped me to ask about the new dog. This in itself was surprising, as I hardly knew any of them. Before I went away, many of the people who spoke to me on that first walk had ignored me. The shop assistants also stopped to admire Biddy and ask questions. I smiled as one of them asked, "Is that one of those blind dogs?" I tried to explain that it was not the dog that was blind, but the assistant didn't seem to see the point.

It is not such an uncommon sight to see a blind person with a guide dog these days, but in 1959 it was pretty unusual. It seemed to me as though barriers began to come down as people stopped me to ask about my dog. As we began to explore more of the area, total strangers would get into conversation with me, perhaps as I stood at a bus stop or waited to be served in a shop. The usual opening remark would be "Oh, what a lovely dog. How long have you had it? How old is it? Aren't they clever?" They wanted to hear how Guide Dogs were trained, and I would answer the endless questions as best I could.

On a number of occasions I was asked to give a talk at various schools in the area, especially the one my children attended. When I was not speaking to schools, I was often invited to speak to other organisations about Guide Dogs, which kept me quite busy for some time. I quite enjoyed myself as I made the rounds. Getting out and about of course added a great deal of interest to my life in general. Staying at home with children did not leave a lot of time for a social life. It was therefore a welcomed change to be able to meet so many interesting people. Biddy certainly created a talking point and I soon made many friends.

It was amazing how quickly Biddy learned our various routes. There were times when I thought she must be telepathic. I used to teach her the name of a shop, or perhaps a person I wished to visit. On leaving home, I would tell her where we were going. I knew that once having been to a place, she would find it again quite easily. The greatest thing about having a Guide Dog was that I could walk out without the stress of trying to find my way around with a white stick. I could walk with confidence down the middle of the pavement without fear of stumbling over something left lying on the ground, or worse, knocking into obstacles and injuring myself on the odd lamp post.

We were not very well off in those early days and as my confidence grew I decided to look for a job. I had been trained as a telephonist but these jobs were hard to come by. I had also been taught to type so I started to look for some kind of secretarial work. The placement officer at the R.N.I.B. was less than helpful mainly because he thought I should not be going out to work with three small children to look after. He also seemed to disapprove of Guide Dogs pointing out that an employer wouldn't take kindly to having a dog cluttering up an office. He made it sound like an official line but I am sure it was his personal opinion. I ignored this sort of bias and started to conduct my own search. I encountered a certain amount of discrimination as I attended the various interviews. The people who interviewed me seemed to have difficulty in believing that a blind person could do anything. Some of the reasons that were given for my unsuccessful application amazed me. The job included other duties that hadn't been advertised. I wouldn't be able to climb stairs. They couldn't spare anyone to take me to the toilet. But finally, after several months of unsuccessful searching, I found what I was looking for. It was only a part time audio typist job in a typing pool but I considered I was lucky to have got it without the predicted objections I had been led to expect on account of my Guide Dog.

I was to work in a large typing pool consisting of about thirty other girls. Nobody objected to having a dog in the office however, and Biddy quickly won the hearts of my colleagues who marvelled at how well behaved she was as she sat beneath my desk.

All was well as Biddy and I slipped into a routine of taking the children to school, going on to work, shopping and various other errands when I finished, then home to housework and cooking dinner for the family.

Shortly after I started work Biddy came into season. Never having owned a bitch before I had no idea of what to expect. This was a very awkward situation to cope with. I needed the dog to get to work and although I sprayed everywhere with Amplex, which is a special spray manufactured to put dogs off the scent of a bitch, nothing seemed to work. One day, I got chased by a pack of dogs all trying to mount Biddy as we walked along. They snarled and growled as I tried to beat them off and the faster I went the worse the situation became as I shouted and tried to shoo them away in an effort to protect poor Biddy. Once they had the scent, there simply was no stopping them. They were all dogs who had been left out to roam the streets at will. Somehow, I managed to get home. I was badly frightened by the experience and decided that Biddy would have to stay home until the season was over. This was only the first of what would be many such incidents. I worried about what might happen the next time she came into season, but I need not have worried however because fate took a hand.

It all started in the following March when I went down with a heavy cold. Consequently, I was off work and at home when

HOME WITH BIDDY

Ricky was brought back from school with German Measles. I realised that I needed to keep him away from other people, especially women who may have been pregnant. He was not exactly ill, so to keep him amused and to keep him out of the way of other people, I decided to take him for a walk with Biddy to a nearby park. All the children were at school and the park was deserted. As he played on the swings and roundabout, I began to feel extremely ill. I cut short the expedition and started back home, but by the time I reached our local shops I was practically in a state of collapse. I couldn't think what had caused the violent stomach pains, the severe headache and dizziness, and the dreadful nauseating feeling of sickness.

By the time I reached the safety of my own home, I was feeling really ill. Over the next few days my condition grew worse and the Doctor diagnosed Gastric Enteritis. Nobody else in the family had been affected and I hadn't eaten anything different from the rest of them so we were at a loss to think how I could have become infected. A few days later I developed Pneumonia and the Doctor sent me into hospital. I was very ill at this stage and not aware of much going on around me.

My eventual recovery took nearly three months and by the time I returned home, my dog had put on a great deal of weight. Before I could start to exercise her properly to get the weight off, I had a visit from one of the trainers at Guide Dogs who was carrying out an aftercare call.

About once a year, a trainer would come out from the training centre to see how the unit was progressing. My visitor was none too pleased with me when he saw how much weight Biddy had put on. I explained about my illness and I also told him about my experience with Biddy when she was in season and the trouble I had had trying to beat a pack of dogs off. After a general discussion, he decided to take Biddy back to the training centre where they would have her spayed. "It would also give us a good opportunity to reduce the dog's weight," he remarked rather sternly.

Obviously, the trainer thought I should have got in touch with the centre when I first became ill. With a sinking feeling, I realised that I was being blamed for neglect. Had I known how long I was to spend in hospital I would have sent Biddy back to Leamington Spa where she could have been cared for properly. I could not expect my mother to take Biddy out everyday as I did, making sure she was properly exercised. She had enough to do looking after the children and running backwards and forwards looking after my home and her own.

Nowadays, all bitches are spayed while they are in training as a matter of course. Even the male dogs, which are being used these days, have their operation before they go to their blind owner. I thank God that I no longer have the worry of a bitch coming into season.

When Biddy was finally fit enough to return to me and I started back to work, I found that things were a little different from how I had left them three months earlier. We had a new supervisor who I am afraid did not like dogs. She made her opinion very clear to me and decided that Biddy would have to stay outside while I was working. In order to keep my job, I would have to go along with this new arrangement but I had many misgivings, and as things turned out, I was proved right.

A quiet corner of the yard was soon found just under the office windows. This was fenced off and provided with a gate, which could be bolted from the outside. Biddy protested loudly the first time I placed her in the run but I took no notice and walked away quickly telling her to be quiet. I went back to the office and sat down at my desk ready to start work. I thought she had accepted her fate because I could no longer hear her protests, but the swing door suddenly opened to reveal Biddy trotting down the gangway, to disappear under my desk. I heard one or two chuckles from the girls seated nearby and the sound of the supervisor's footsteps approaching. "You'll have to take the dog back," she said irritably, and then added, "management orders." I stood up and placed the lead back on Biddy. Reluctantly I retraced my steps and returned once again to my desk. I barely had time to sit down before the door was flung open once more and Biddy came running down the gangway wagging her tail as if to say " Hello, I'm back."

This state of affairs continued throughout the week and I was becoming seriously worried because I thought I might lose my job. Indeed, I thought it highly probable if the supervisor had anything to do with it. I decided to contact the Guide Dog Association to ask for their advice. A trainer came out from the centre immediately and soon had the situation in hand. Standing well out of sight, he quickly discovered how she was making her escape. By putting her paw over the top of the gate, she was managing to push the bolt, which was on the outside, far enough back so that it swung open. He recommended the gate should be made higher to prevent further escapes. This did not stop Biddy who seemed hell bent on proving how resourceful a Guide Dog could be. As soon as she discovered she could no longer get out by her previous method, she dug a hole underneath the gate. This was quickly dealt with but the noise that she made as she howled to be allowed back under my desk went to everyone's heart and bread rolls, sandwiches, cakes, plus biscuits and anything else edible began to cascade into the run. Having solved one problem, it was swiftly followed by a further complication as Biddy tried different tactics. When she found that escape was no longer an option, and that all was lost, she decided that perhaps we wouldn't go to work at all that day. Every morning I had to wrestle with her to get her into the run because she sat down by the gate and absolutely refused to budge. When she lost this particular battle she tried another tactic. As I walked down the road towards my offices I suddenly began to realise that people were coming towards me and passing me. It was not until I met one of the girls who sat near me that it occurred to me that I must have walked straight passed the entrance. I can only think that Biddy must have done it deliberately and hoped I wouldn't realise that we had gone by.

Eventually, the situation was resolved as complaints filtered down from the management about the dreadful noise Biddy was making as soon as she was left in the run. Within two or three weeks the embargo was lifted and she was allowed back into the office to the relief of everyone who thought I was being unfairly treated just to satisfy the whim of someone who was not particularly fond of dogs.

Shortly after this incident I was faced with an upheaval of a different kind. We had been living in our prefab for ten years but in the sixties when the town planners went mad and started tearing the centres of towns and cities apart, they also decided to pull the prefabs down and re-house all the council tenants. A new estate was going up and everyone was on the move.

Many of our neighbours were moving to different parts of the town but others moved, as we did, on to the new estate.

The winter of 1962-63 was particularly harsh. Right after Christmas Eve it started to snow in Luton. That was the beginning of the big freeze, and the thaw did not come until March. This was a very difficult time financially for us because my husband was in the building trade and could not work during this period. Snow conditions made getting around hazardous to say the least, and I shall always remember the kindness of our doorman who used to keep a bowl of warm water ready to wash the salt from Biddy's paws as we arrived for work each morning. The roads were so bad that half the time the buses were unable to run and I had no option but to walk. Many times I slipped on the ice or staggered through a snowdrift but Biddy worked like a Trojan and we usually arrived in one piece. I dislike cold weather at the best of times but apart from the difficulties of trying to get about, we were experiencing trouble at home with burst pipes, power cuts and a shortage of money to buy coal. The last straw was when the tank burst in the airing cupboard and the water flooded the bedrooms and hall. As it was so cold, the water froze on the floor thus making it possible to pick a sheet of ice up in one go before it did any damage and put it outside. When the thaw eventually came, we were on the move to a brand new three bedroom council house on an estate, which was still being built.

As the snow disappeared and the roads and pavements once again became visible, I realised that the new estate was virtually a building site. Biddy coped with all the bricks and planks of wood left lying around and guided me safely past cement mixers and other obstacles associated with the building trade. We also had to get used to the new surroundings. We were further away from where we had previously lived and this meant that I had to go further afield for shopping and the boys also had further to go to school. Work on the estate had been delayed because of the bad winter. This meant that no pavements had been laid and I had to walk in the road. Life was made even more difficult for me as I tried to cope with the conditions by the volume of heavy lorries supplying the building site. Gradually, things became easier as pavements were laid and building debris disappeared. I was to spend ten years on this estate during which time we were to have an increase in our family when I gave birth to a baby daughter in 1965. Unfortunately, she was born prematurely and consequently was left severely disabled due to lack of oxygen. Nowadays, doctors can regulate the flow of oxygen and prevent tragedies of this kind happening, but sadly medical science had not reached that point when my daughter was born.

This was a particularly difficult and upsetting period in my life but if I hadn't had the benefit of my Guide Dog, who took me backwards and forwards to the hospital for six months, my life would have been much more difficult.

Biddy served me faithfully until 1967. I remember her with special affection because she was my first experience of owning a Guide Dog and learning what a difference a Guide Dog can make to the life of a blind person.

The full extent of my daughter's disability was only just beginning to register when I found the lump on Biddy's back. Eighteen months had elapsed since I gave my job up when my daughter was born. Now I had to face the possibility of a further crisis.

HOME WITH BIDDY

With a sinking heart, I made an appointment to see the vet. I was horrified to learn from her that she thought the lump might be a tumour and wanted to operate. Realising the seriousness of the situation I hesitated to give my consent. We agreed that I should get in touch with G.D.B.A. before any final decisions were taken and see what advice the trainers at Leamington would offer.

They proposed that one of the trainers should collect Biddy and take her to a veterinary college for a special x-ray. She was duly picked up and taken away. A tumour was diagnosed and she was operated on. When the operation was over, she was brought back to me, but on consideration, the trainer decided not to leave her with me because she still had stitches in her back. Poor Biddy was taken away once more and that was the last time I was to see her.

Lady luck was not smiling on me at that particular time because it was discovered that Biddy also had an eye disease which was only diagnosed when she was taken back to Leamington. Sadly, nothing could be done to save the eye, which had to be removed. I was very upset when the Guide Dog Association broke the news to me. I would have to wait until another dog became available before I could retrain. In fact, it was five months before I was called in for a second time.

I have many treasured memories of Biddy and when she was taken away, it was the end of a wonderful partnership. When I finally went back to Leamington to train with my next dog, whose name was Lassie, I was pleased to learn that Biddy had been found a nice comfortable home in Exeter where we had started out together. During the time I was at Leamington,

I met the lady whose parents were now caring for Biddy. Over the next few years the lady was kind enough to keep in touch with me, and let me know how Biddy was progressing. Biddy lived on in happy retirement for a further three years before her heart failed and she died.

CHAPTER FOUR

LASSIE TAKES OVER

The Guide Dog Association still had a waiting list in 1967 although they tried hard to give priority to replacements where possible. I was to wait five months before a suitable replacement was found for me. This time I would be training at the Leamington Centre, which was much nearer home.

Family circumstances had changed since I trained with Biddy. My parents had moved to the coast so there was no help I could call on as I had when I trained at Exeter. As the boys were older now and therefore not so dependent on me, they were obviously not such a worry, but as I would have to be away while I trained, special arrangements would have to be made for my young daughter to be cared for. The five months I spent on the waiting list I found completely frustrating. Losing Biddy was like losing one of the family, and I missed her so much. Any Guide Dog owner will tell you what a wrench it is when your dog has to retire and you have to get used to another dog. Unfortunately, a dog's life span is not as long as ours, so every time my dogs have retired, I vowed I would not go for another. Each time of course, I gave in and retrained because I have experienced the comparative ease of getting about. It is true that I had the odd accident, but had I not had the advantage of owning a Guide Dog, I am convinced I would probably have come to grief many more times than I actually did. In spite of the difficulties of being away for the duration of the training, I decided to go ahead and accept another dog.

The extent of the damage done to my daughter by the lack of oxygen was becoming all too apparent. I put her slowness to develop normally down to being premature. We had been told that she was blind and that her nervous system had not had a chance to completely develop before she was born. My husband, Bob, and I were heartbroken at the prospect of our only little girl not being able to walk, and also very upset by the added disability of blindness. We were to find out later that she was also somewhat retarded but we were grateful for the fact that she could speak properly and could hold a conversation.

I set about finding the professional care she would need while I was training because she obviously could not be left with anyone even if they had offered. The R.N.I.B. ran a Sunshine Home just down the road from the Guide Dog centre in Leamington. I was aware of this from my previous visit to Leamington so I asked the Social Services to arrange for them to take Susan in for the short time I would be otherwise engaged. Fortunately for me there was no difficulty in arranging for the Sunshine Home to look after Susan. This was a great load off my mind especially as I was assured that I would be welcome to visit her every day.

The physical effort of trying to cope with family duties and care for a premature baby began to take its toll. Bob preferred to ignore the fact that the baby would never walk or see. He was never one to help much in the home and it seemed that I was always left to cope with everything. Our marriage was being affected by all the stress but it wasn't until 1974 that we finally made the break and finished up with a divorce in 1976.

That however is a different story, which it is not necessary to go into here.

By the time I arrived back at the Leamington centre in January 1968, the Association had expanded. Two new centres had been opened, one in Bolton in 1960, and the other at Forfar in Scotland in 1965. More and more blind people were applying for dogs. Thanks to the efforts of the Blue Peter children's program on BBC TV, which helped to publicise the work, and the generosity of the general public, the Association was becoming one of the richest charities in the country, even though there was no financial support from the government. Obviously, in order to meet the demand for new applicants and replacements, the Association needed to have a regular supply of dogs available at all times. A suitable supply of dogs had always been a matter of concern to the Association until 1955 when a breeding program was introduced. In 1960 the Association was able to develop and expand its breeding program still further by opening special breeding kennels at Tollgate House.

Just after the First World War when the advantages of a dog as a guide for the war wounded men who were returning home was recognised, only German Shepherds were used. Over the years, however, other breeds have been found suitable for the work such as Labradors, Retrievers, Collies and a variety of crosses. The favourite cross these days is Labrador and Retriever. Most of the dogs being used up until then were either purchased from breeders and members of the public, or they were donated. Any dog accepted in this way had to meet a number of requirements. It had to be the right height, have a good temperament and possess a higher level of intelligence than normal, apart from not being shy in heavy traffic conditions. These were only some of the attributes required before a dog could be accepted, it still had to be tested further as soon as it was brought into the Centre before it started the initial stages of training.

I joined my companions with mixed feelings wondering if this time round I was going to be as successful with the new dog as I had been with Biddy. At least, I thought, I had done the training once so I knew what to expect. Not much had changed as far as I could remember. Students were always addressed formally as Mr. or Mrs., and the instructors were always addressed in the same way. Although students were addressed as adults, we were not allowed out on our own even if the student was quite capable of getting around. This ruling did cause some muttering among some of the male members of the class who wanted to nip out to the pub occasionally. Those who wanted to soon side stepped this ruling by ignoring it and armed with their long canes they would slip out and enjoy a couple of pints at the nearest pub. The rest of us decided to bite the bullet, buckle down and get on with the course. We were expected to be ready for training promptly at nine o'clock in the morning and to be available in the evenings to attend lectures on animal care and animal health. Students were expected to be on time for meals but if you failed to appear, someone would quickly come looking for you. It was a bit like being at school all over again but not quite as bad because there was always the dog.

The class numbered ten and although we got off to a bad start, things soon improved. I need not have worried however because the newcomer turned out to be just as intelligent and faithful as her predecessor. This was just as well because we were to spend the next nine years together. Lassie was an approved dog. This was surprising since I knew that the Association bred most of their own dogs and no longer needed to take in dogs from outside. I also knew that even if she had been donated, she would have passed through a rigorous training program. She was not a pure black Labrador but was crossed with a Collie and perhaps something else as far as anybody could tell.

We were given our dogs earlier than usual because there had been a heavy fall of snow during the first night of the class. We were unable to do much work on the handle the next day, as conditions underfoot were too dangerously icy. The trainers thought that the weather was too bad for man and dog alike. There was plenty that could be done inside so the class set to and waited for the weather to improve.

As far as I could remember the training had not changed. Most of us were replacements. This meant that those of us who already had a dog, would probably be able to complete the course in three weeks instead of a month, if all went according to plan. During my first week however, I was convinced that someone had made a mistake and not matched me properly with the dog. Lassie showed very little inclination to work for me or even to like me very much. I found that she was very nervous and would bark at the least sound, I tried hard to bond with her but she stubbornly ignored me until I really thought that we were not meant for each other. I spoke to the trainer about Lassie and he said that we were doing fine and to stop worrying. He said that I was probably comparing the new dog to the old one and that I should concentrate more on bonding with Lassie instead of looking back to Biddy.

I have since learnt that every dog is different. As with people we are all individuals and it is just the same for dogs. Each one of my dogs have been completely different characters, and it is precisely this that makes them so special. In Lassie's case, she was a very timid little dog and therefore inclined to be quite nervous, but as soon as I realised this, we started to get along just fine.

Although I got off to a bad start, the training period slipped past quite quickly. As expected, most of us were through in three weeks. Before leaving the training centre I went for my final interview with the controller. I would have to sign a special agreement for my dog and pay the obligatory 50p.

As I left the training centre and said goodbye to my class companions, I wondered how long it would be before I was back again. I went home feeling grateful that at least, for the immediate future, I had regained my independence. Lassie soon settled into her new environment and in next to no time we were out and about visiting friends, shopping, keeping appointments and generally doing all the things I used to do with Biddy.

As I went about my various errands, I would often be stopped by a complete stranger, who would ask me the same questions people used to ask when I first returned home with Biddy.

"Hello," would come the greeting, "what a lovely dog, you have there. That isn't Biddy, is it?"

"No," I would answer patiently, "this is my new dog."

"Oh," they would say in amazement, "I thought it must be. How long have you had this one?"

"Only a short while," I would explain, "but we're getting used to each other." The next question would be "What's her name?"

"Her name is Lassie," I would reply.

"How old is she?" and then they would stop a minute longer to tell me how wonderful they thought Guide Dogs were and what a marvellous job they thought Guide Dogs did.

On occasions I would have the opportunity to meet other Guide Dog owners in the area. Most of them were leading very busy professional lives. I remember a physiotherapist working at the hospital, and a lady who travelled to London every day where she taught music in a school in the centre of the city. Another lady worked in a bank and someone else I knew worked in a factory. All very busy people going about their daily lives with a loyal shadow at their side. At the end of the sixties, there was something like two thousand units working in the country.

As I settled down with Lassie I began to think of more outside interests. Whilst at school I had learnt music and I had kept my interest over the years. It had only been a pastime up until then, but I now decided to turn what had only been a hobby to good use since I could no longer go out to work. There was only one way I could increase the family income and that was by playing in pubs and clubs. There was a certain social aspect to this occupation which I enjoyed and because I needed to be out in the evening and not during the day, it meant that Bob could do the baby-sitting rather than have to pay someone else to do it.

The boys were growing up fast and when Susan went to special school, life became a little easier at home. I began to look for more interests outside the home. It had to be something I could do during term time. I eventually enrolled at the local college of further education as a mature student to do O-levels and A-levels. Relations between Bob and myself had been strained for some time. We had disagreed over the years on a number of important issues especially where the children were concerned. His attitude towards women was totally outdated and because he had received very little in the way of education himself, he saw no value in it whatsoever. "You must be mad to want to go back to school at your age," he told me angrily. "You should be here looking after us." I ignored his outbursts and settled down to try to achieve something worthwhile.

I did my best not to allow my activities outside the home to interfere with family life. Unfortunately, I was constantly criticised and deeply hurt by the many cutting remarks hurled at me, nothing I did was ever right. Bob became resentful and often morose with a tendency to lose his temper over the slightest thing that went wrong, while I would argue in retaliation, or in self-defence, thus becoming extremely frustrated and more and more miserable.

With every passing month the situation grew worse. As a married couple, we were going nowhere. The final break came one foggy October evening in 1975, which resulted in me leaving home for good. My sister had recently taken over a pub in Aylesbury with her husband, and my parents had moved back to be near her as my father's health was failing rapidly. I therefore made my way to Aylesbury to break the news that I would be seeking a divorce and to throw myself on their mercy since I was now homeless. My parents only had a one bedroom flat and so it was my sister and brother-in-law who finally came to the rescue and offered me a home.

I was in a strange town where the only people I knew were my immediate family. I did my best to make myself useful around the pub helping with chores wherever possible. I started to explore the town with Lassie. Although I had passed through Aylesbury on my way to school and back home on numerous occasions, I knew next to nothing about the place. During those first few weeks Lassie and I often got lost but we were quickly put right when I mentioned the name of the pub. We soon found our feet however, but it was a very unhappy time for me.

Apart from putting down roots in a strange town, I was desperate to maintain contact with my sons, and especially with Susan who was now at school near Kettering. Once a fortnight, Lassie would accompany me by bus and train to visit her. She soon became a favourite among the children who were delighted with her, hardly allowing me time to get in the door before enthusiastically gathering round to pet and fuss her.

During school holidays we travelled backwards and forwards to Luton by bus to visit her while she was home. When she moved schools again, we travelled up to Shropshire to visit. We made trips to London and went all over the place looking for work. Had I not had the help of my old friend at this particular period in my life, things might have been very different. With Lassie's help I managed to maintain contact with my children.

Shortly after settling in Aylesbury my father died, leaving my mother on her own. She told me that she didn't want to stay in the flat she had shared with my father but was going to ask the Council if she could move to sheltered accommodation. We agreed that I should stay with her until such time as she was able to move. The arrangement suited both of us because I was also able to help her over the loss of my father, which she took very badly.

In spite of all my efforts, I was unsuccessful in finding work and decided to go back to college to continue my studies that had been interrupted. I used my musical ability once again and found myself a job in a pub playing the piano. I was also able to help my sister who needed someone to play the organ for a sing along in the pub on a Saturday evening. What little money I earned in this way I put aside to save in the hope that I would eventually be re-housed. I had already applied to the council with this in mind but I was informed that as there was such a long waiting list, I stood next to no chance.

During those early years in Aylesbury, I relied heavily on my Guide Dog. Lassie was a fast learner and could go to any shop I chose to name without hesitation. One particular incident sticks out in my mind. Although I can smile about it now, at the time it caused me much embarrassment.

On several occasions I had visited a certain hairdressers. As I was less than satisfied with the service I received, I switched my allegiance to another hairdresser further up the road. Two different hairdressers shared this particular shop, one on the ground floor, and the other on the first floor. I chose the one on the first floor, which obviously entailed climbing the stairs to keep an appointment. The previous shop had no stairs, as it was simply a small place divided into gents' one side and ladies hairdressing the other, both sections being at ground level.

I had quite a long walk into town but on this particular morning, I was going to be very late for an appointment. Lassie and I started rushing along the road to try and make good the time. I was going so fast that I tripped up a curb as I tore along and fell flat on my face. Scrambling to my feet once again, I felt the blood trickling down my leg from a nasty graze on my knee. Determined not to be late for my appointment, I grabbed the harness and, annoyed with myself, I said to Lassie in a very impatient voice, "Hairdressers!" We continued on at almost jogging speed, eventually arriving breathless at the shop. One of the girls took my coat and I told Lassie to find the stairs. "Excuse me," the young assistant said, "but what did you say? I thought I heard you tell your dog to take you up some stairs, but there aren't any stairs here dear." she said kindly. I took a deep breath and asked the assistant the name of the shop. When she answered, I knew that I had gone to the wrong hairdressers. My confusion was complete when the young lady said sympathetically, "It looks as though you've hurt yourself, would you like me to bathe your knee?"

A year was to pass before my mother was given sheltered accommodation. I moved back to the Prince of Wales where Lassie once again joined my sister's poodles.

The pub was tucked away down a country lane well away from the main thoroughfare. It was surrounded by fields and situated near the canal, which made it a favourite watering hole for fishermen. In order to reach the pub I had to walk down a very quiet country lane, as there was no public transport. Often I would hear a rustle in the hedge and a low murmur of a cow on the other side. Noises I couldn't identify always made me nervous. I would urge Lassie on, and quicken my pace so that I arrived home as soon as possible. I have nothing against cows, I'm sure they are wonderful creatures but large animals make me feel very nervous at close quarters. I once made a four mile detour after a motorist stopped me to tell me a cow was loose in the lane.

It was often necessary to ring the nearby farm when cows invaded the car park or when one got loose in the lane. One of Lassie's less endearing habits was to disappear through the fence and find a cow pat to roll in, returning home smelling decidedly high. This meant that we had to tether her in the car park and hose her down before allowing her back inside, an operation she was none too fond of.

Living at the Prince of Wales had its social side. If I got tired of my own company in the evenings when my sister and her husband were downstairs busy in the bar, I would often join the regulars for a leisurely drink and a chat about the old days. The older locals would delight in telling stories about some of the things that used to go on at the Prince of Wales.

The pub dated from 1820 and was originally a coaching

inn. When the railway was built and came through from Cheddington to Aylesbury it ran right across the road where originally there was a level crossing just outside the front door of the pub. The railway then continued on to pass the back door. As the line fell into disuse, it was never removed before being covered with concrete and still lies beneath the road and car park to this day.

The locals used to tell us about the old railway workers who would stop the engine when they reached the pub, deliver a few shovelfuls of coal to keep the pub fires going and in return receive a pint on the foot plate from the grateful landlord.

Occasionally, I had the opportunity to meet one or two celebrities who would just pop by if in the neighbourhood looking for an out of the way pub where they could enjoy a quiet drink. I remember John Paul, an actor who often appeared on TV. He used to make me laugh when he did the voices of the various characters he portrayed in plays.

One day, an artist came into the bar and presented my sister with a painting of the Prince of Wales. She was evidently impressed with the artist's efforts because she bought the painting and hung it where it could be easily seen and duly admired. She told me later that she had seen a young man sitting outside with his easel but had not dreamt that he was actually painting the pub.

Saturday evenings were the busiest night of the week. We used to have a good crowd in who enjoyed singing along with me as I played their favourite songs. Over the weeks word spread and the Prince of Wales seemed to become a popular place for many hard working people looking for a night out. I was soon able to identify those customers who would approach me asking me to play their particular favourite song every time they came in. I made several good friends during the time I was playing at the Prince of Wales. As time went on, I was heartened to learn that people were coming along especially for the entertainment. It was secretly gratifying to feel that I must be making quite a name for myself.

Unfortunately, Lassie did not share my fans' enthusiasm for music. If she happened to be in the bar as I prepared to sit down at the organ, she would come over to me, give a loud sniff, touch my hand and disappear quickly behind the bar. The very next time the kitchen door was opened, she would make good her escape, leaving us in no doubt of her opinion that she obviously considered the music an unpleasant noise to be avoided.

Lassie did not enjoy being among a lot of strangers all trying to pet her. She was inclined to be nervous and timid. I rarely kept her in the bar with me knowing that she didn't like crowds, but on the odd occasions when she was with me there was always a danger that people might feed her without my knowledge.

Labradors are notorious scavengers and when in training it is impressed upon Guide Dog owners not to allow well-meaning people to feed their dogs. We were warned against the dangers of titbits, which are very bad for working dogs. Not only does sneaking food to a Guide Dog have the effect of distracting the dog by drawing its attention away from its owner, but it also makes the dog put on weight. It is essential that Guide Dogs keep healthy so a strict eye has to be kept on the dog's weight. For this reason, owners are required to visit their vet every six months for a health check just to make sure the dog is in good condition.

By 1976 Lassie was nearly ten years old and showing signs of age. On one of our regular veterinary health checks my vet advised me that Lassie was developing a little kidney trouble, "Nothing that can't be controlled." she told me. She suggested that Lassie should wear a little coat over her back in extra cold weather, or if it was especially wet. She also put her on a special diet and asked me to bring a urine sample in as soon as possible. I gloomily thought of how I was going to manage to put a container underneath my dog at the crucial moment. "Get someone to help you." the vet answered when I asked how I was to obtain the desired sample. As I left the surgery she called gaily, "Have fun! I'll see you soon."

If you have ever undertaken this particular task, you will know just how difficult it is. I enlisted the help of a friend and while I held Lassie on the lead, she was to pop the container beneath her as soon as she began to squat. The trouble was that Lassie did not co-operate. Lassie seemed to think that Anne was offering her a drink in the container and kept trying to stick her nose inside it. Each time Lassie began to squat, Anne would creep up and try and place the container, and every time she failed because Lassie just stood up. We collapsed into laughter at our ineptitude but after many attempts we finally managed to collect a dribble which I proudly took back to my vet.

Fortunately, there wasn't much wrong and Lassie was just kept on her special diet. I followed the Vets advice and bought Lassie a little coat. She didn't mind wearing it at all and when we finally parted company, I kept it as a keepsake and still have it to this day.

I have another keepsake from my time with Lassie. While I was at college, I joined a pottery class. Using Lassie as a model, I produced her in clay proudly wearing her harness. When my efforts were completed, the instructor surprised me one day by asking permission to place my work in an exhibition. Lassie was on show for some time before being transferred into yet another exhibition. The model now sits on my dressing table where I remember my little friend every time I touch her.

Another year rolled by before Lassie was to retire. This happened quite suddenly in the following year and came as a shock to me because I had no idea that there was anything wrong. On one of my regular visits to the vet, Lassie was found to have a cataract in both eyes. As she was now eleven years old and due for retirement, I was asked to send the harness into the centre immediately. From then on I would have to manage with Lassie on a lead and a stick until such times as I was called for training.

I badly wanted Lassie to stay in Aylesbury so that I didn't lose contact with her. I set about finding her a suitable home and at one point I really thought that I had succeeded. I was due to go on holiday and just before I left, the person I had chosen changed his mind. This left me with no option but to ask the Association to re-home Lassie since I was in no position to handle two dogs. I was still living at the Prince of Wales, and my sister already had two dogs of her own. My brother-in law thought that four dogs would be too much of a good thing. I doubted whether I would be able to manage two dogs even when I had accommodation of my own.

Early in September I received two letters, one from the Guide Dog Association telling me they now had a dog available for me, and the other from the Council informing me that a flat had been allocated to me.

Everything seemed to be happening to me at once. A week before I left for Leamington, a spot of romance was to creep into my life. No one knows what the future might hold for them. I certainly never dreamt that the man who came into the pub that evening and engaged me in conversation would later become my second husband.

CHAPTER FIVE

MY LADY AIRLIE

In 1977 G.D.B.A. reached yet another milestone in its development when it opened a fifth training centre at Wokingham in Berkshire. The demand for dogs was still outstripping the supply. New applicants were coming forward all the time requesting training but the existing necessity for replacements still had to be met as working Guide Dogs grew old and retired.

My visit to the Guide Dog Association in that year was largely uneventful. It seemed that very little had changed in my absence apart, of course, for a number of new faces among the staff who were strangers to me. I learned that one of the newcomers was to be my instructor. He introduced himself as Mr. Hamilton as students were still expected to address the instructors by their surnames. Kenny Hamilton had been transferred from the Forfar Centre in Scotland and had brought with him six dogs, four of which were destined to join their new owners on the class of ten students.

I was pleased to learn that I was to be allowed to keep Lassie with me until my new dog arrived on the scene. It was not until the Sunday morning that I said a very painful goodbye to my old friend. As she walked away with the kennel girl who had come to collect her from my room, I wished with all my heart that it had been possible to keep her at home with me. After having given me so much in the way of independence, companionship, and wholehearted loyalty, I felt a deep sense of betrayal knowing that I would probably never see her again. I wondered miserably if the new dog was going to like me, or even if I was going to love her as much as I had come to love Lassie.

A few minutes after Lassie's departure, there was a knock on my door and the instructor came in with my new dog. I suspected that he had been waiting for Lassie to leave before bringing Airlie in to meet me.

After a brief introduction he stayed a few minutes to tell me a little of Airlie's history. He described her as a very pretty little yellow Labrador with beautifully expressive brown eyes. She was nearly two years old and he added kindly that I would probably find Airlie very different from Lassie who was now very old and a great deal slower than Airlie would probably be.

"Airlie had been puppy-walked in Scotland by a school mistress", Mr. Hamilton began, as he sat down to chat. The lady was a friend of his and he told me how she used to take Airlie to school with her to join the children in the classroom. The teacher had encouraged the children to join in various fund raising projects, which they did with great enthusiasm. They apparently all adored Airlie and were now waiting for a photograph of her with her new owner, which they would receive at the end of my course to hang on the classroom wall. Airlie had been christened after Airlie Castle and Mr. Hamilton told me with a smile that he believed that as Lord and Lady Airlie were also enthusiastic supporters of Guide Dogs, this little fact might have influenced the choice of name.

While we had been chatting, Airlie had been examining the room with her nose but when Mr. Hamilton got to his feet to leave she immediately sprang to attention. He ignored her and turning to me he said, "You stay here for a while with Airlie and start getting to know her a little. Later, you can come downstairs at break time and we'll all have a little talk about how you got on. Don't get Airlie too excited though, just talk to her quietly" he advised. So saying he edged his way to the door and was gone. As I listened to the sound of his footsteps fading away along the corridor I considered myself fortunate to have such a nice instructor and I felt confident that my training would be successful with Mr. Hamilton in charge.

Airlie didn't seem to mind being left with me. She returned to examining her new surroundings while I made light conversation hoping to attract her attention. Eventually, she came over to me and proceeded to examine me with her nose as thoroughly as she had been sniffing round the room. Finally satisfying herself, she climbed onto the dog bed and prepared to snooze.

As we were all replacements we were able to qualify after only three weeks. I was anxious to get back home as quickly as possible as there was much to arrange before I could move into my new flat. I left the training centre with Kenny Hamilton's words of advice ringing in my ears. "Don't forget your dog is going into a strange environment, and she is going to need your support," he advised me seriously. "I expect lots of your friends and your family will be anxious to meet the new dog, but you must keep her quiet at least for the first day. It wouldn't be fair to take her out on the harness until tomorrow. You must allow her time to get used to her new home first. Anyway," he added cheerfully, "I shall be over next week to make sure you have both settled down okay."

I said a cheerful goodbye to my fellow students and left the centre without any misgivings, confident that I could pick up my life more or less as before. My circumstances had changed slightly and I looked forward to the prospect of living and coping independently.

I returned to the Prince of Wales and was surprised to learn that I was not the only one on the move. My sister Joan, and Les, my Brother-in-law, had been offered another pub and had decided to accept it. The Partridge Arms at Aston Clinton was just outside Aylesbury but there was a good bus service, Joan told me, so there was no need to worry, I would still be required on a Saturday evening to do the usual sing-along. This pub had two bars and a function room, which they hoped to open as a restaurant. The move would probably take a few weeks to arrange but until then it would be business as usual at the Prince of Wales.

My flat was situated on a council estate within easy reach of the town centre. Fortunately, it was on the ground floor with a pocket of garden at the back, which could easily be fenced off for the dog. There was a regular bus service, which stopped just outside the front door and a couple of shops on the corner of the road. My family was relieved to know that I at last had some accommodation but regretted that the area was notoriously rough. Beggars can't be choosers, I thought, and prepared to move in as soon as possible counting my blessings as I started sorting things out.

The man who had taken my job over while I was away became a regular visitor to the Prince of Wales on a Saturday evening. He would sit by the organ as I led the sing-along and talk to me about his interest in music. He told me his name was Norman and that he came from Manchester originally. Shortly after my return he asked me if I could help him. He explained that he had taken a job on at a club on a Friday evening but felt that he had bitten off more than he could chew. He asked if I would consent to accompany him to help him with the entertainment when things got busy. In return, he would give me half the fee and make sure I got home safely. I thought it over carefully before agreeing but finally accepted thinking that if nothing else it would be a social night out. Despite my initial reluctance to take Norman's invitation seriously, over the next few weeks leading up to the Christmas period we became good friends. He was the kind of person who seemed to know everyone. Because of his local knowledge of pubs needing live entertainment, he was able to put a few more playing jobs my way for which I was very grateful.

Airlie settled down surprisingly quickly. When I left the training centre she was still under two years old and retained much of her puppy playfulness. One of her favourite pastimes was to grab the end of the broom as I attempted to sweep the floor. If I put a brush or a duster down it would quickly vanish. I had to be careful to shut drawers and cupboard doors properly because if I didn't I would find the contents strewn round the floor. I also discovered that Airlie had a passion for things that flapped, and this tendency was to lead to trouble in the future. I soon learned to take precautions but many of the items I lost during those early days remain lost to this day.

I knew from experience that it was going to take a little time before I felt as confident with Airlie as I had done with Lassie. I soon became very fond of my new friend as we grew to know one another better. She was just as good on the harness as Lassie had been but she was a completely different character. Airlie showed no nervousness and hardly ever barked where Lassie would bark at the least sound and was very wary of people she did not know well. Airlie was much better than Lassie when confronted with a group of children when I had occasion to visit schools to give a talk. Lassie had never wanted the attention of the children who wanted to fuss her whereas Airlie was quite ready to play games. This was not surprising given Airlie's history. Lassie had been an approved dog and probably never puppy-walked in the same way as Airlie. Although I felt that Airlie was quicker at picking things up, I also remembered being advised not to compare dogs because they are all different.

As I went about the town it was not unusual to be stopped by someone who wanted to know if I had a new dog now. "Where is the black one?" they would ask. When I got onto a bus the driver would often remark on Airlie and I would be questioned all over again. "That looks like a different dog," the driver would say, "I thought you had a black one, is it a bitch or a dog?" he wanted to know. "How long have you had this one?" I would be asked, quickly followed by the next question, "How old is she?" and then the driver would remark, "She looks lovely, what's her name? Is she as good as the old dog?" The questions would continue with all the passengers on the bus taking an interest. "What happens when your old dog retires?" I would be asked. I would have to explain that Lassie had to retire because she was gradually going blind with cataracts and that she also had a little kidney trouble. "Do they put them down when they're to old to work any more?" I would be asked. Then I would have to go into details of how the

Association kept a list of people willing to take retired Guide Dogs and that they would quickly find her a new home. It seemed as though I answered the same questions a thousand times. However, we soon got known as we went round the town. Airlie quickly learned the various shops I used and she also learned the way to the different places I visited on a regular basis.

I often took her with me if I went out playing. She usually became the centre of attention. Customers would always want to feed her and I had to be really strict about people giving her things that were no good for dogs, such as crisps. During our training we were warned about the general public feeding dogs. If I wasn't careful, the odd treat would be slipped to her without my knowledge. The Association was very strict on this point because dogs could easily become overweight and develop heart problems if the rules weren't strictly kept. I would patiently explain why it was so bad to give a Guide Dog treats only to be met with "Oh but she is so friendly and she's looking at me with those lovely eyes and pleading for a bit." The danger of strangers feeding Arlie while I was working in unfamiliar pubs wasn't the ony reason to leave her behind at my sister's pub...

One evening while I was busy doing the usual sing-along I suddenly discovered that Airlie was missing. I knew that Airlie had become quite friendly with the landlord's dog whose name was Rebel. He was a German Shepherd and very popular with the customers. Although Rebel was allowed to roam freely in the pub, I always kept Airlie's lead looped around the organ stool so that she couldn't wander. Rebel often went walkabout to visit a second pub run by the landlord. Evidently, that particular evening he had shown Airlie the way and they had gone off together. However, before any harm could become either one of the dogs, a customer from the Crown walked in with both dogs telling us that they had arrived unaccompanied and so he had brought them back.

After that particular incident I decided to leave Airlie with my sister if I went out playing in future. I was horrified when I considered the route the dogs must have taken through the town. Over busy roads and right through the main square before arriving at the Crown. The landlord didn't seem at all worried. He thought the whole thing very funny and said how intelligent Rebel must be to show Airlie the sites of Aylesbury on a Saturday night. He told me that Rebel went walkabout quite regularly but I felt so guilty when I thought that Airlie might have been knocked down and badly injured.

In the following March, Airlie was once again in trouble.

As it was a nice day I had left the window open in the sitting room but when I went to close it I found a large lump of nylon curtain missing. It didn't look torn but the edges were ragged as though someone had tried to cut it. Frantically I looked for the missing piece but failed to find anything. When Norman called in later that day, I asked him to take a thorough look round the garden but although there were a number of holes where Airlie had been digging, there was simply no sign of the missing piece of curtain. I became uneasy with the growing suspicion that Airlie's fascination for things that flapped had been too great to resist and she had pulled the curtain down and swallowed it since, search as we may, there was no trace of it to be found.

Any dog owner will tell you that dogs are apt to devour the most unappetising titbits. I had heard from a friend of mine that her Guide Dog had eaten her nylon tights and had to be rushed to the Vets for an emergency operation to remove them. Other Guide Dog owners had told similar stories of dogs eating socks and other items of clothing.

I lost no time in rushing to the vets who confirmed my worst fears. After examining Airlie the vet said that she could feel the curtain inside her and added seriously that it would probably mean an operation if she couldn't get it out under anaesthetic. She told me I was to bring Airlie back the following morning. I was instructed not to feed Airlie that evening but the vet said that she could be permitted a little water if she wanted it. This was a bit hard on Airlie since she was a true Labrador and loved her food, but I was very worried and determined to do as I was advised.

The next day I left Airlie at the vets and went to visit my

mother where I spent the next few hours anxiously waiting until it was time to ring up for the results. Just before the appointed time the phone rang. I was speechless from the blow I received from that telephone call as I replaced the receiver. It wasn't from the vet, but was to tell me that my second son had been involved in an accident at work and was believed dead.

Later that day I somehow took in the information that the vet had been successful in extracting the curtain from Airlie's intestines without the need of opening her up. She recovered remarkably quickly from the experience but ever after, I always made sure that my curtains were tied back so as not to flap in the wind.

The next few weeks were very difficult for me. It took me some time to regain any sense of normality after the blow I received on that fateful day. I longed to be with my remaining sons and my daughter to comfort them and perhaps gain some strength from them to help me bear the loss of a twenty-three year old son with everything to live for, and with the rest of his life before him. This was not possible however, because of the rift that still existed between my ex-husband and myself. We had not parted amicably and not even the death of Ricky had done anything to heal the breach.

Six months were to pass before Airlie once again gave me cause for concern. In September of that year my eldest son Peter came to spend a holiday with me. One day he took Airlie out for a free run, while I busied myself with household chores. He was soon back however, calling to me urgently as he came through the door to call the vet immediately. I dropped what I was doing and went to find out what had happened. While he had been running the dog, Peter explained to me, a van had drawn up and the driver had let two German Shepherds out of the back. One of the dogs had made a beeline for Airlie and attacked her with disastrous effect. It had practically torn her ear off and it was pouring with blood. As she shook her head she sprayed us generously and however hard we tried to stop the bleeding, we could do nothing to help.

Peter had tried desperately to defend Airlie. Failing to drive the dog off, he had lifted her in his arms. This however had not stopped the attack and Airlie had wriggled free only to be set upon once again. Eventually, the owner came across to call the dog off and to apologise when Peter told him that Airlie was his mother's Guide Dog and that he would make sure that he paid any veterinary bills.

I rang the vets only to be told that they could not come and collect Airlie. I was advised to get a taxi but I pointed out that Airlie was bleeding badly and I doubted whether any taxi or bus would allow me to travel even a comparatively short distance to the vets. After a certain amount of pleading on my part, I finally managed to persuade the girl on the other end of the line to relent. Briefly conferring with a colleague, she reluctantly agreed that she would arrange for someone to collect Airlie.

Poor Airlie looked like a wounded soldier when I went to collect her. Her head was bandaged and she was also wearing a bucket so that she couldn't scratch her ear and pull the stitches out or pull the dressing off. For the next two or three weeks Airlie spent the time feeling very sorry for herself. While she still wore the bucket, she couldn't see round corners properly and consequently kept bumping into things. Obviously, with such a contraption on, I was unable to work her.

When the vet finally decided that she could leave the bucket off and just have a bandage, Airlie demonstrated just how quickly she could remove it. I had to make regular trips to the surgery for the dressings to be changed and on one occasion I had only just got outside in the street before the vet was running after me telling me that I would have to return because the dressing was already off.

As soon as I was able, I began working Airlie in harness. She still had stitches in her ear so the bandage remained round her head. This was a great talking point and Airlie revelled in the attention it attracted. Whenever I got on a bus the driver would ask why she was wearing a headdress. I became heartily sick of having to explain to people what had happened. It was a relief when the stitches finally came out and the bandage was removed.

Shortly after this incident Norman and I decided to get married. The wedding was to take place in the following January. I wanted to get Christmas over first because I expected to be busy playing for the inevitable Christmas parties and any other celebratory gatherings that might require my services.

I was sitting quietly one evening when Norman turned up unexpectedly. "I've brought your wedding present," he informed me. There was a funny squeaking noise coming from the direction of his coat. I was curious to know what it could be. "Come and have a look at this," he invited. I found a little fluffy head sticking out of his coat and further exploration revealed a tiny kitten. I was enchanted as I relieved him of his charge and cradled the little creature in my arms.

Somehow, I had never been able to keep a cat. Every cat I had owned had either got lost or run over. I wasn't particularly looking for an addition to the family, but having once seen the kitten, I was sold. It was a female cat and I christened her Perdy. I was to keep her for the next nineteen years.

I am not sure who adopted who, but Perdy certainly adopted Airlie as her mother, and Airlie played the part right from the start. How she ever put up with Perdy's antics I'll never know but she was patient and long-suffering as only a Labrador knows how to be. Norman often laughed when he spotted Perdy walking underneath the dog or when she mounted an aerial bombardment on Airlie from the top of the settee or other piece of furniture as long as it was high enough. Airlie even allowed her to come sniffing round her food bowl and also to sleep in the basket with her. As long as Airlie was about, everything was all right according to Perdy. She certainly showed no fear of dogs. On one occasion, a big Labrador called Henry came to visit us and we were startled to hear him whimper. When we looked to see what was wrong, Perdy was discovered under the chair playing with his tail every time he wagged it.

Bucks is a pleasant county with plenty of country walks around Aylesbury. We loved to take advantage of good weather and get out in the fresh air where there was no fear of traffic and we could wander at will while Airlie had a free run. One day, we chose to take a walk along the canal. Airlie spotted a moorhen sitting on a bed of weed in the middle of the canal. She went straight in after it and sank with the weed. She came up looking like the Loch Ness monster with weed hanging from her ears. As she clambered out and shook herself a friendly passer by stopped to watch as Norman tried to get some of the messy wet weed off. He smiled as he told me that he had seen the dog jump straight into the canal after the moorhen and had never seen anything quite as funny as when she came up with weed hanging all over her. I remarked that I didn't think it was very funny and the smell was no laughing matter either! Norman only laughed at my turned up nose and said that it was a pity he hadn't brought his camera with him.

We left the canal and started down a lane allowing Airlie to free run so as to dry off. It was then I suddenly realised where we were. Airlie recognised her surroundings before I did. The Prince of Wales where we used to live was just down the lane. Before I could stop her she had raced into the car park and up the steps. Somebody opened the bar door to leave the pub and Airlie went straight into the bar.

No doubt Airlie had expected to find her dearest friend Les behind the bar waiting to welcome her home. What she found was a very disgruntled landlord who wasn't very pleased to see her at all. "Is this your dog?" he asked crossly as we came through the door. "I can't have it in here in such a state, you will have to take it outside." Airlie stood there in all her glory laughing up at the landlord. I was very embarrassed but I could see his point. Airlie smelt dreadful and she was still dripping water everywhere. I tried to explain that we used to live at the Prince of Wales and Airlie must have thought she had come home. However, the landlord was having none of it. He told us to leave immediately but Airlie took a bit of persuading. As far as she was concerned, she had come home and she was staying.

Whenever Joan and Les went on holiday, Norman and I became caretakers at the Partridge Arms. We would take up residence while they were away. A manager came in to run the bar so we didn't have to worry about that side of the business.

I usually managed the cleaning, looked after the poodles and did any shopping needed for the kitchen.

The pub garden was very open with only a small wire fence between the pub and the next house. It was also broken in several places, especially at the top of the garden where there was a wooded area. It was quite easy for the dogs to get through and we often had to go and round them up in the woods. The poodles were no bother, they never strayed far, but Airlie would wander off and it often meant a full scale search before we found her again.

One morning while we were busy cleaning the bar I noticed that the poodles had come in but Airlie had once again failed to return. I asked Norman if he would go and have a look for her before she strayed too far.

Norman wandered up the garden and spotting the man next door in his garden he asked him if he had seen a yellow Labrador. The man replied furiously that he had seen the dog and now had it shut in the shed. He told Norman that he was about to get his gun and shoot the dog. Wondering what could have happened, Norman asked why Airlie had been shut up. "You see all these feathers," the man shouted, "that dog of yours has just killed my three prize bantams!" When the man learned that Airlie was a guide dog he was even more angry and Norman hurried in to fetch me. I had an awful time trying to calm the situation. There were feathers everywhere and there was nothing I could do to bring the three bantams back that Airlie had killed so swiftly. I could only apologise and offer some kind of compensation. I knew my dog had done wrong and I told the man I would get in touch with the Guide Dog Association immediately. I begged him not to harm her but to release her promising to keep her in from now on. I wept with relief when he finally let her out of his shed and she came bounding back over the fence.

As a result of this little escapade, Guide Dogs wrote to the man offering apologies and compensation but pointing out that Labradors were really gun dogs and that Airlie had just been following her instincts. When off the harness a Guide Dog is the same as any other dog, but of course, this didn't make it right. The public do not always take this into account because of the high profile the dogs have. When Joan and Les returned we pointed out to them that we had probably lost them a customer. Joan told me that one of the poodles had recently done the same but she had seen in time before any harm had been done.

Shortly after this incident we moved from the flat into a bungalow. The only one who objected to the move was Perdy. For three days she sulked refusing food or comfort. When we let her out into what passed as a garden, she would disappear. Stories of animals finding their way back to an old home would cross my mind. Norman had brought her from the flat in the car so I thought it unlikely, but you never know! I sent Norman back to the flat just to make sure several times but there was no sign of her. Obviously, she was hiding somewhere but as soon as Airlie appeared in the garden, Perdy was never far behind. It was obvious that Perdy felt secure as long as Airlie was in sight. She kept this behaviour up for about three months but finally gave in and decided to stay with us.

Airlie and I quickly adjusted to the new surroundings. Although we weren't too far from where we used to live, we were no longer on a good bus route nor were there any convenient shops nearby. The estate was still in the process of being built but we soon learned to avoid the places that might have proved difficult.

On returning home from town on the bus one day, the driver put me down at the wrong stop. This completely threw me because I thought I was where I should have got off. Consequently, I finished up disorientated and lost. There was no one around to ask for directions so I decided to keep walking until I either found a familiar area, or I could ask assistance from the next person I met.

Giving the command "forward" and telling Airlie "home" we set off. Strangely, we headed across a field but I thought Airlie knew where she was going so I kept walking. We reached pavement again and shortly after, tail waving vigorously, Airlie headed up a path. In a flash, familiarity took over and I knew where I was. I had come home all right - back to the flat.

I tried again but still with no success. Whenever I told Airlie "home" we landed back at the flat. I decided to try a different tack. This time I said "let's go and find Perdy." I had completely lost my bearings and after walking for over an hour Norman suddenly appeared at my side and spoke to me. "Where on earth have you been until now! I was getting quite worried." I was so grateful that he had come to find me I could have wept. I asked him if he had the car with him and he replied "Yes, it's right here." I put my hand out and opened the car door. This somewhat surprised him and he asked where I thought I was going. "Home, of course." I replied preparing to get into the front seat. "You ARE home!" he told me.

Now I am more familiar with the area I understand what probably happened. I found the whole experience very upsetting apart from the fact that I felt such a fool. I learned later that I was not the first to have experienced getting lost. It had happened to other Guide Dog owners I spoke to but from then on I always made quite sure I was getting off the bus at the right stop.

I met a number of people during the eighties when the electronic organ was becoming very popular. In my roll as entertainer I often came across a number of hopefuls who had bought organs and on getting them home, found they needed a bit of help to play them properly. I would go to the person's house to teach them on their own organ and we often became good friends. I have good reason to remember Anne in particular as I grew to know her quite well in this way. One day, she invited Norman and I to share Sunday lunch since it was Easter. As this was to be a special occasion, turkey was on the menu. My friend had a dog of her own and asked me to bring Airlie as the family wanted to meet her.

The visit started off fine and everybody enjoyed the Easter lunch our hostess provided. After the meal my friend suggested that I should give her a quick lesson. As I left the room with Anne I thought that the dogs would be all right together while I was busy. Regrettably, unknown to me, someone shut them up together in the kitchen while the rest of the family watched a programme on TV so that we would be left in peace.

Peace was shattered after the lesson finished and Anne went into the kitchen to make a cup of tea. She was horrified to discover that she had left half a turkey on the worktop, along with various left over food which included a salad intended for Sunday tea. Anne was furious and said that they would all have to have egg and chips for lunch the next day because the dogs had eaten the turkey. Unfortunately, we will never know which dog was guilty. Moosh and Airlie sat gazing at her with big doggy eyes, the picture of innocence.

Once again, my sweet little Guide Dog had managed to embarrass me. I tried to apologise but Anne told me pointedly that her dog never stole. She added in a very aggrieved voice that she thought that Guide Dogs were trained not to do that kind of thing. Knowing a Labrador's appetite, I never left food out where Airlie could get it. I was too polite to tell her that I thought it was her own fault for leaving food unattended. Needless to say, our friendship came to an abrupt end, as shortly after this incident Anne told me that she wouldn't be taking any more lessons because she was starting her own business and would not have time.

During the latter part of the eighties, Norman's health began to deteriorate quite badly. Emphysema was diagnosed and things would only get worse. He felt he could no longer cope with moving the organ around to venues so we decided to sell it and join up with a friend of mine on accordions leaving Norman to do the vocals. This worked for some time but even this grew too much and my colleague and I often had to do without his services.

On several occasions, Norman would have to spend a short stay in hospital and I would have to cope on my own. It never really worried me but time was passing and Airlie was beginning to show signs of age. In 1987 when I was visited by a trainer for an after care check, he suggested that as Airlie was now twelve years old, I should start thinking about another dog as Airlie was well overdue for retirement.

Here we go again, I thought desperately. This time, I was

determined to keep Airlie near me. I knew I couldn't keep her and manage with two dogs. Many couples are able to keep the old dog by allowing the partner to take it over. This would not be possible for me because at this stage, Norman could hardly walk.

Usually, the Association recommends Guide Dogs should be retired when they are about ten years old. This is to allow them a little time to live as an ordinary pet. When the time comes, the owner has three choices. They can either keep the dog, take the dog back to Leamington and ask them to find a new home for it, or they can find a home for their dog with family or a friend.

Norman didn't want me to go for another dog. He knew that it would mean that I would be away from home for at least three weeks. He was reluctant to be left on his own. I had to insist and point out that if he died before me, which of course was highly probable, I would be left with no means of mobility and I was certainly not prepared to be without the means of getting about safely.

By the time I was informed that there was a dog available for me, I had found a new home for my old friend with Kevin and Karen who were anxious to find a pet for their young daughter. They didn't want a puppy and were delighted at the prospect of having a retired Guide Dog.

I knew the couple quite well. At the time I was involved in an organisation for disabled artists and Kevin was one of our helpers. Karen often joined us, bringing Emma with her. Emma was fascinated with Airlie and they were delighted when I took them up on their offer to re-home Airlie. I was relieved to think that I would be able to see her at least once a week. Karen told me that she was on a course and would sometimes be away for the weekend. I told her not to worry. I would always have Airlie home if necessary. I was determined to do the thing properly and we arranged to visit Karen and Kevin at home to let Airlie get used to the new surroundings before she went to live with them permanently. They lived by the canal where there were always plenty of ducks paddling to and fro and I couldn't help remembering when Airlie had taken a dive and gone after that moorhen.

By the time I was ready to go back to Leamington, Airlie was an old lady of thirteen years old. She told me quite plainly that she was tired and too old to work any more. When I put the harness on, she would hardly move, but when the harness was off, she would walk at a normal pace. Clearly, it was time for us to part.

Airlie was not quite finished with me yet. The day before she retired she managed to cause me embarrassment once more just for luck.

Norman had gone to keep a hospital appointment and I was busy in the bedroom packing a case ready for the morrow when the gas man called to clean the gas fire out. This was done with a noisy vacuum cleaner, which Airlie took exception to. He made quite a lot of noise also as he worked and I think he must have frightened her with all the banging around he was doing. When the gas man had finished and packed his equipment ready to leave, I opened the door to let him out. One minute Airlie was standing beside me, and the next minute she had bolted. Desperately I stood and called with no success. In the end I asked a neighbour to help me. We trudged around for about an hour before I rang the police. After a while they rang back to say she had been found. Norman was less than pleased when he came home. When we got to the police station, I explained what had happened. I wished the floor would open and swallow me up when the officer said that he didn't think Guide Dogs did things like running off. Then he added insult to injury when he told us that there would be a charge of £3 before I would be allowed to collect her from the dog pound.

Had she been wearing her collar with her medallion which held her address, she might have been returned to me without further trouble, but of course, she only wore the play collar when she went free running. These days, Guide Dog owners are advised to keep the play collar on all the time just in case the dog should stray. The medallion has the dog's number on it and as soon as the loss is reported, the owner can be traced immediately.

The general public appear to regard Guide Dogs as wonder dogs. It is because they look so smart, and they are admired for the job they do. It should never be forgotten however, that they are dogs first before they become Guide Dogs. That is what makes them so endearing to their owners, even if they do cause embarrassment at times, just like any ordinary dog.

CHAPTER SIX

TOGETHER WITH MERRY

9th September 1988 - eleven years to the day, I was back at the Leamington training centre ready to train once again with a new dog. Nothing seemed to have changed in my absence, only the welcome addition of a bar in the centre was new where students, kennel staff, apprentices and instructors could meet in the evenings on an equal footing and get to know each other in a more relaxed and social atmosphere.

The programme looked set to follow its usual pattern. There were ten of us on the class this time and my instructor was to be Mr. Thompson. Most of my fellow students were back for a replacement apart from one gentleman who was a first timer. Two things stick out in my mind about that class.

The class always started with an introductory talk given by the instructors in charge. A young lady was brought into the room and introduced to us. We learned that her name was Kate and that she was an apprentice. The trainer told us that she was wearing blinkers. As part of the training would-be Guide Dog trainers have to undergo, she was expected to endure twenty-four hours in blindfold to experience for a short time what it was like to be blind. The poor girl was certainly thrown in at the deep end and all the students agreed that we would take care of her during this period as the trainer asked.

She had been collected from the centre of Leamington and brought into the building with the blinkers on. She got the guided tour of the building just like the rest of us. She was also expected to cope with the daily business of eating meals, dressing and toiletry, and finding her way around the building. She would generally be treated as a student to help her understand what it was like for a blind person coming into a strange place for the first time.

Kate was very good and did all she was asked to do. In the evening, some of us played scrabble with her to pass the time and keep her entertained. All the little counters have Braille letters on them and also a raised print letter, which could be easily felt. She managed to get the idea very quickly and we all enjoyed the game. The blinkers were due to come off at twelve o'clock the next day. We all stood round Kate counting the seconds down to zero hour. It must have been a tough test and I admired the way she had coped. She had joined in with us and done all the things we had to do. As soon as the blinkers were removed, we gave her a cheer and asked her how she felt. She told us what a blessing it was to be rid of the blindfold and see light again. She said she felt very disorientated and needed a few minutes to register her surroundings. What a shame, I thought a little enviously, that we all couldn't take our blinkers off. We were stuck with them but we wished Kate the best of luck in her chosen career as she left.

The dogs were allocated the next day. I was given a Labrador Retriever cross whose name was Merry. I clearly remember Mr. Thompson saying as he brought her in to me, "Merry would like you to think that she was a tough little cookie, but underneath, she is a very sensitive little soul." In the weeks to come, I was to find out just how sensitive she could be.

As Mr. Thompson slipped quietly out of the room leaving me alone to get to know my new companion, I sat on the floor stroking Merry's head. She was a Labrador Retriever cross not a pure Labrador. I knew that the association was always experimenting with different breeds and crosses, but now they were using a number of Lab crosses because it was considered that the mixed temperament of each breed gave the best results. She was bigger than Airlie but as soft as silk and I thought fleetingly of the future wondering how we would get on.

Our first night together proved very disturbed. I woke to what sounded like an old man coughing. There was an alarm in the room but just in time I remembered we had been warned not to touch it unless there was a real emergency such as a fire, or even a heart attack. He explained that the alarm would go off in everybody's bedroom and therefore the entire staff would come rushing to see who needed help. Apparently, the staff had responded to the alarm on several occasions only to find a Labrador sitting on the window-sill where the alarm was located, or they had been disturbed in the night because a student couldn't find something they were looking for.

I gradually realised that it was Merry who was coughing and I got out of bed to see what I could do for her. I gave her water, which didn't seem to help because she kept the coughing up half the night as well as being very sick. I cleaned it up and decided to wait until morning before reporting Merry's ill health.

When the class assembled promptly at nine o'clock the next morning ready to start training and the trainers asked politely if we had all slept well, I spoke up and reported the events of the night. "Oh, it is only kennel cough!" the trainer told me, "It's just like us having a bad cold. We'll get her some antibiotics and she will be fine." I was overruled when I voiced my opinion and said that I didn't think Merry should be expected to work in her condition. I had never heard of the effects of kennel cough before but I knew how infectious it was. Probably all the dogs would go down with it before long but nevertheless, the trainer was adamant, nothing was going to be allowed to get in the way of the training programme.

I need not have worried. Merry did recover fairly quickly but, as expected, some of the other dogs went down with kennel cough but were kept in class. Kennel cough sounds dreadful and is very infectious, but if treated in the early stages it is easily cured. Apart from this minor problem at the beginning of training, everything went according to plan and I was home again within the three weeks.

Norman picked me up from the centre and we drove home. On arriving, I expected to find Perdy waiting on the doorstep. In fact, she was in the hall as we opened the front door. She looked at Merry and stalked straight passed us. She obviously knew that I had not brought her dearest friend Airlie home and she was going to let us know just how disappointed she was. Perdy never really accepted Merry in the same way as she had Airlie. As far as Perdy was concerned, Airlie was her mother. She never slept in the dog bed with Merry, and she never walked underneath her for protection as she had often done with Airlie. Occasionally, Perdy would walk up to Merry and meow straight in her face as if to say, "Who are you?"

The first few weeks of a new partnership are always a bit of an adventure. There didn't seem to be any problems, Merry settled down very quickly. She was good in the house, good in the car, got on well with the cat simply by ignoring her and learned the various places I frequented comparatively quickly.

The only thing she took exception to was the dog run. We had had this specially put in and gated at both ends. The front gate was the gate that normally led to the garden, with a path running down the side of the bungalow. We had chain link gates put on the other end to fence the side in so that the dog could not escape.

Merry hated being shut in the run. I couldn't understand how she kept getting out. We decided to watch and I didn't believe that a dog could climb up chain link but it was true because I heard her, and as she climbed she cried because the hard chain must have hurt her paws. We soon cured her by putting an extra piece on the top of the gate, which prevented her from jumping over the top.

The dog has to take in a great deal of new information as the owner teaches the new dog all the familiar routes so recently made easy by the old dog. You never quite knew what might happen. My first surprise came one day as I negotiated my way round the bus station. As I passed a bus queue, a mother moved a pusher out of the way so that I could get past. There was a distressed cry from the child as I went by and I thought that the little one was probably frightened of dogs. "Don't worry dear," I said, "she won't hurt you." The mother put her hand on my arm and said "Excuse me, your dog has just stolen my little boy's cake."

I was very embarrassed and offered to compensate her. The mother refused my offer but as I hurried away feeling very humbled, a lady standing in the queue turned to the mother and observed, "I didn't think Guide Dogs did that sort of thing." That well remembered phrase seemed to follow me as I walked away. How often had I heard those words. I was to find out in the weeks to come what an expert scavenger Merry could be. This was not the only incident of what I used to refer to as hoovering on the hoof. Unfortunately, little children in pushchairs are at nose level and Guide Dogs are not supposed to steal the odd ice cream out of the mouths of babes.

I remembered being told that the Association bred Labrador-Retrievers, especially to keep the best qualities of each breed. Well! I certainly knew from experience how greedy the Labrador could be, now it seemed Merry could also show the stubborn streak often found in the Golden Retriever. First she climbs the fence, now she was scavenging. What next? I thought desperately. I wondered if she had inherited the worst traits of each breed, but I wasn't going to let her beat me.

None of my dogs had ever shown the least fear of fireworks. Therefore, I was very surprised at Merry's reaction on Guy Fawkes night. I remembered what the trainer had said about Merry being sensitive as I tried to calm her hysterics. There was nothing I could do to comfort her as she panted and shook with fright. When I put her food down for her, she wouldn't touch it. This was serious, I thought, whoever heard of a Labrador refusing food? I knew many dogs were afraid of fireworks and I always kept any animal in my care well away from any danger on bonfire night. When I consulted the vet, she suggested that I gave Merry a tranquilliser if she got too bad. I wasn't keen on doing that because it would mean that I couldn't work her for twenty-four hours until the effects had worn off.

After that, I always dreaded the approach of 5th November. Merry's fears didn't stop at fireworks however, she reacted in just the same way to hot air balloons. Unfortunately, balloons are a common sight around the Aylesbury area. Thunderstorms also had the same effect on Merry. In fact, on one occasion, she actually passed out in a thunderstorm. I really thought she was dead and I was about to ring the vet when she stirred. Apart from the odd occasions when she displayed this kind of paranoid behaviour, she was a great little worker and I grew to love her just as much as I had loved the rest of my dogs.

I spoke to the trainers about Merry's nervousness when they came out to visit me on one of the regular aftercare checks. Although they were sympathetic, they just reminded me that lots of dogs were frightened of fireworks, and even farm animals didn't like hot air balloons. Of course, they argued, we don't get many balloons in Warwickshire. They pointed out that thunderstorms never lasted very long and they were sure I could cope with all the little problems troubling Merry.

It was getting near Christmas and one day I caught the bus into town intending to do some Christmas shopping. Merry tucked herself under the seat out of the way of trampling feet. The bus stopped and the inspector got on, but as the bus moved off again, Merry shot out from under the seat barking furiously. All the passengers on the bus started to laugh as the inspector made his way up the aisle, saying, "Tickets please." I was at a loss to know why Merry was barking and why her hackles were up. A lady sitting near me told me that the inspector was dressed up as Father Christmas and that she supposed Merry didn't like him.

When we reached town and I attempted to get off at my stop, Merry wouldn't go past the Inspector who was standing at the door. Tongue in cheek I suggested that the Inspector might like to get off first and walk away so that I could calm her down and persuade Merry that it was safe to leave the bus.

A few days later, I was standing in a bus queue in the bus station happily chatting to the lady standing in front of me. As usual, I was answering questions about the dog as we waited for our bus. Within a few minutes a bus drew into the stop and everyone got off. Suddenly, Merry stood up hackles raised and started barking furiously. As this behaviour was most unusual I turned to the lady standing near me and said "My goodness! Anybody would think Father Christmas was on that bus." The lady burst out laughing and replied, "Well! How on earth did you know that."

Obviously, Merry didn't like people dressing up. There were other instances when she took exception to people in funny costumes like the time I was buying a ticket for a show and Donald Duck wondered through the foyer. I hurriedly left the premises with Merry still barking as we went down the slope outside the building.

On another occasion I was unwise enough to take Merry with me to a play which was about bouncers who threw people out of discos when they were misbehaving. In the first scene the bouncers began dragging a young man out kicking and shouting. Merry stood up and gave vent to her disapproval of such bad behaviour by barking loudly. I thought any minute I would be asked to leave but the audience started laughing. Every time the action on stage involved somebody getting thrown out, Merry would start barking right on cue, and the audience loved it. As I sat cringing in my seat, from somewhere behind me I heard a lady remark to her companion, "Aren't those blind dogs clever, they even train them to act." Merry kept her objections up all through the performance and by the end of the play, I believe the audience thought that she really was part of the act.

When the cast came on to take their bow at the end of the performance, they clapped the dog and the audience added to my embarrassment by joining in. After the show I was asked to join the cast in the bar for a drink. I laughed and joked with the cast expecting any minute to hear that well-worn phrase, "I didn't think Guide Dogs did that sort of thing.", but this time I was wrong. That generous cast only laughed and said what a buzz they had got every time Merry barked, and how clever they thought she was to come in right on cue. Where had I heard that people in the theatre always said that they should never work with animals and children?, I asked myself. After that experience, I privately vowed never to take Merry to the theatre again.

During the early months of 1988, Norman's health had begun to deteriorate quite badly. He had already suffered one heart attack in the June of that year but by the time I came back from Leamington, he seemed to have recovered sufficiently. In March of the following year however, he took a turn for the worse and had another heart attack. It seemed to be down hill from then on. In July when the temperature soared into the nineties, he went down with pneumonia and went into hospital on the Monday, but by Tuesday afternoon, he was dead.

After ten years of marriage, I was alone again with only a dog and a cat for company. Although Norman's health had been giving cause for concern for many months, his death was still unexpected at that time and therefore a great shock to me. I took comfort from the thought that I had not listened to him when we discussed whether I should train with another dog.

I had never really stopped looking for work but three weeks after Norman's death I was asked to attend an interview for a job. It was the biggest surprise to me when I was given the job of telephonist to a well-known company in the town. That job came at just the right time for me because it meant that I wouldn't have to sit at home alone but could be with colleagues at work. On the appointed day, I duly presented myself with Merry ready to take up my duties.

Merry was an immediate success in the office - at least she was until the lunch hour when I took her out for a run. I chose a spot that I thought would be safe, not realising that it was bounded by a brook. Merry found the water and decided to go for a swim. She came out smelling atrociously and dripping water. I was obliged to take her back to the office in a quite disgusting state and apologised for her condition, as I had nothing to dry her off with. I was so embarrassed I could cheerfully have strangled Merry. What a way to start a new job I thought miserably but nobody in the office seemed to be worried. Merry, on the other hand, proceeded to demonstrate just how pleased she was with her exploit by shaking herself vigorously and showering anyone standing too close with dirty water.

Since Merry had come on the scene, I had made every effort to keep in contact with Kevin and Karen who were now looking after Airlie. I smiled when Karen told me she had christened Airlie, Lady Airlie, because Airlie clearly did not consider that she was a dog. Each week I would attend a local Art Centre where I had become involved with a group of disabled people. The group had formed into an organisation to promote and provide opportunities for disabled artists of all kinds. Kevin was one of our helpers and he would bring Airlie to our weekly meetings so that I could see her. There was no problem with the dogs, they were great friends right from the start.

One day Karen asked me if I would mind looking after Airlie for the weekend while she went on a course. I was delighted and agreed immediately.

Airlie was getting very old by this time. She was now fifteen years old and going deaf and blind through old age. When Karen brought her on the Friday evening, I wasn't too surprised to learn that Airlie now had to be fed by hand, otherwise, Karen explained, she couldn't get her to eat anything.

The dogs got on fine together and immediately Perdy saw Airlie she seemed to recognise her. Perdy never got into Merry's bed, but as soon as Airlie climbed into her basket, Perdy climbed in after her as though she had been there all the time.

I duly followed instructions when it came to feeding time. I put Merry in the run while I fed Airlie. I had to coax her and this took some time but eventually I was able to let Merry in for her feed. I put the bowl down on the floor and told Merry to fetch. I heard her go to the bowl, but then I heard her whimpering. When I looked to see what was wrong, there was Merry sitting behind Airlie who was gobbling Merry's food as fast as she could get it down her.

To say the least, I was so surprised since I had stood for at least fifteen minutes hand feeding Airlie trying to coax her to eat a little, and there she was, tucking into Merry's food and showing very definitely who was boss round here.

A few weeks later, Airlie gave me cause to be very proud of her. One morning the telephone rang and when I answered, my friend on the other end asked me if anyone had told me that

Airlie was front page news. I had to admit that I knew nothing of this and asked what had happened. "Oh! Airlie has saved the life of a dog that had been tied up and left in the canal to drown.", she told me excitedly. The story ran that Kevin had been walking along the canal path with Airlie running ahead. She had started to bark furiously and ran back to Kevin obviously asking him to follow. She ran to a spot where the water was very shallow and when Kevin looked down, he saw the dog with its back legs tied together in the canal.

Kevin was able to clamber down and reach the dog. He pulled it out and cleaned it up as best he could while Airlie tried to lick some life back into it. With Airlie running at his side, Kevin carried the dog to the police station because it was so weak it couldn't stand, and explained how he had found it. In no time the story was in the local paper. RETIRED GUIDE DOG SAVES LIFE OF DROWNING DOG were the screaming headlines. The dog was taken to the dog pound, the same place that Airlie had once been taken. We found out later that the poor creature had arthritis in its back legs but good came out of the situation because the dog was found a new home where it was looked after and loved for the rest of its life.

Airlie died in the following year aged sixteen. That was a very sad day, I felt that I had lost a dear friend. She was thirteen when she retired and therefore enjoyed three years as an ordinary pet and I thank Kevin and Karen for making those years happy for my Lady Airlie.

In the early nineties, the Association opened an hotel at Teignmouth where Guide Dog owners with their friends and families could spend a holiday. All facilities were laid on for the dogs so the owners didn't have to worry about carrying dog food, feeding bowls and dog beds etc. I was quick to take advantage of the opportunity to spend a short break at the seaside. I had a friend who was also blind but did not have a Guide Dog. I asked her if she would like to come along and feeling very adventurous, we set off for Teignmouth.

When we reached our destination Merry must have thought we were back at the training centre because there were so many dogs around. In some cases, where a couple were both blind, they each had dogs. In other cases, where maybe a family member was unable to leave a pet dog, they also brought them along. Runs were provided in the grounds, and a grooming room set aside in the hotel. The food was left ready in lockers and the bedrooms were provided with dog beds. There were kennel staff on duty round the clock, and a police cadet on duty ready to help where needed. You couldn't ask for more and whenever anyone asked me where I was going for my holidays, I would tell them that I was going to a special hotel for Guide Dogs, where they let the owners in if they were good.

My first visit to Cliffden Hotel was not the success I hoped. I had only been there for a couple of days and really enjoying being able to get out in the fresh air. Most of the guests tended to gather in the bar in the evening. On this particular evening we were all in the bar with the dogs when the cadet suddenly noticed that there was something wrong with Merry's eye. She had also been coughing and sneezing a lot that day. I called the girl on kennel duty who suggested that Merry might have kennel cough, but she was also concerned about her eye which looked very nasty. She arranged for me to take Merry to the vets' the next day. The vet was also very concerned about Merry's eye and advised me to see my own vet as soon as I returned home.

TOGETHER WITH MERRY

He couldn't really make a diagnosis but gave me some cream to use on her eye so that it didn't become inflamed. He also advised that Merry should be isolated from the other dogs just in case she infected them with suspected Kennel Cough.

I spent a very worrying week unable to get out very much and wondering what would happen when I got home and saw my vet. Although the staff at the hotel were all very kind, that is one holiday that I would rather forget. I have been back to Teignmouth many times since that visit and always enjoyed the time I spent there. At any given time there are approximately twenty-five dogs in the hotel. Special walks are arranged for them where they can run free, and be ordinary dogs for a short time, and they love it.

On my return home I saw my vet immediately who diagnosed an eye condition known as Hornis Syndrome caused by a muscle becoming paralysed. The Kennel Cough turned out to be hay fever, which came as quite a surprise to me. It was not so surprising though when you consider how near the ground a dogs nose is and all the constant sniffing around it does. The vet told me that the eye might right itself in time but she wanted to keep a close watch on it because of the danger of infection. In fact, things went back to normal after three months of trotting backwards and forwards to the vet. On the other hand, the hay fever cleared up pretty quickly.

As Merry grew older, her phobias became worse. Hot air balloons were particularly difficult to deal with. We get lots of balloons in the Aylesbury area and I always knew when one was around. Merry would start reacting by shaking and trying to hide. Even if I was in a car and there was a speck on the horizon, she would begin to shake. Sometimes, when I asked if there was one about, my companion would say there were no balloons up and shortly after, one would appear far away in the distance. Merry seemed to have a sixth sense where hot air balloons were concerned which never failed to amaze me. How is it possible for a dog to know that the balloon is there when it is high up in the sky and miles away and she is travelling in a car? I know that many animals get frightened by the hiss of the gas when it is released, and farm animals have been known to stampede when one is overhead, so it is not surprising that farmers get annoyed when their livestock get upset.

If ever I happened to be out with Merry on the harness when a balloon was about, Merry would stop and refuse to go any further. Then the shaking would start and I would have to ask a member of the public to help me get home practically dragging a terrified dog between us. On another occasion, Merry turned herself completely round and started to run back home with me holding on for dear life. I was sometimes asked if my dog was properly trained and I would embarrassingly explain that she was indeed trained, but at the moment she was very frightened.

Obviously, Merry was not puppy-walked in an area where this problem occurred. She was puppy-walked in Warwick where there were no hot air balloons that might have got in the way of aircraft from Birmingham passing nearby.

I faced the same problem when it thundered. Merry would start shaking hours before the thunder could be heard. She would turn to me for comfort when the storm got bad and would try to climb up on me begging me to save her from the unknown terror. I remember how frightened I was when she collapsed in a thunderstorm. I had never heard of a dog passing out or fainting, on this occasion there was a terrific clap of thunder overhead. Merry was standing just behind me in the bathroom, refusing to move from my side. The clap made me jump and I knocked the soap container into the bath, which made a further crash. Merry dropped to the floor and lay there without moving. My mother happened to be staying with me at the time and I called to her desperately to come quick. There must have been a lightning strike somewhere near us because when I asked my mother to ring the vet, the phone was out. Merry was far too heavy to lift so I sat on the floor talking to her and stroking her. I thought she was dead until my mother told me that she had opened her eyes. I was so relieved and when I told my vet she said that it was not unusual for sensitive animals to die of fright. "In future," she advised, "you had better give her a tranquilliser when thunder is forecast." This was difficult because it meant that if I tranquillised Merry, I would be unable to work her for twenty-four hours because she would be too woozy.

My mother happened to be staying with me on another occasion when I was invited to a garden party to celebrate the fortieth birthday of one of our club members. As there were going to be tables set out in the garden for the meal, our friend asked the members with dogs not to bring them in case the tables got knocked, so I left Merry with my mother. Just before the end of the evening, thunder started rumbling away in the distance. I wasn't worried at that stage hoping I would be home before the storm broke. However, it came on very fast and before we could get away, the storm was upon us. The drivers decided to wait until the worst was over so I just had to sit it out and be patient. When I finally got home sometime later, my mother was having hysterics because Merry had trapped her in a chair, and when she had finally managed to get free and go to bed, Merry had got into bed with her. My mother was ninety-three at the time, a very frail old lady. When I reached home she was in tears, and trying to hold Merry off with her walking stick.

I had to take charge of the situation and calm my mother down. I put her to bed with a hot drink. Mother was so exhausted that she was soon asleep which was just as well because I could then turn my attention to Merry who was still having hysterics. This was not easy because she refused to be comforted. I shall never forget that night because it was five o'clock in the morning before the thunder stopped and I finally got some sleep.

The third great fear was of fireworks. I dreaded Guy Fawkes night, and the few weeks leading up to it. Many people have said that the tradition should be banned, and judging from the trouble it causes, I agree wholeheartedly. Not only does it frighten pets, but many accidents are caused to children who play with fireworks unsupervised. I have always made sure that any animal in my care on that particular night, are safely shut away from danger.

The only time I ever knew Merry to refuse food was when she heard a firework go off. It didn't matter how far away the bang was, Merry would start whimpering and shaking. There was nothing I could do to convince her that the thing was nowhere near and therefore couldn't hurt her. I had to be careful not to open any outside doors when she got in to a panic because if I did, she would just bolt.

My worst experience of Merry's panics was one day when I got off the bus a short distance from my home. Some boys nearby let a firework off and Merry tried to bolt. She bolted into traffic dragging me with her. Horns started to blast and a car braked suddenly just behind me but no one came to my aid. Somehow, I got to the other side of the road but found myself completely disorientated and lost. There is never anyone around when needed so I just kept going until I found a road sign I was able to read because of the raised letters. This acted as a landmark and I eventually found my way home.

This incident frightened me so much that I decided that something would have to be done. I had had enough at this stage. I loved my dog dearly but I thought that if I didn't act quickly to stop her panic attacks, I stood a good chance of landing up dead. I therefore got in touch with the Association who agreed that Merry should retire. This could not happen straight away however, but I started looking for a new home for her in the nearby area - somewhere I could keep in touch with her in the same way I had been able to keep in touch with Airlie.

Merry now lives happily in Winslow with a friend of mine who has two daughters. The family love her, and she is now away from those horrible hot air balloons because the flight path does not go over Winslow. I see her when Chris brings her into Aylesbury and she has met my present Guide Dog whose name is Fable.

Merry and I were together for nine years. She was a wonderful little worker when things were quiet but I know she had her faults. Unfortunately, there is no such thing as a perfect Guide Dog. They are a wonderful mobility aid but it should never be forgotten that they are dogs long before they ever become a Guide Dog. Each one is different and should be loved for themselves.

CHAPTER SEVEN

FABLE

I planned to take my holiday with Merry down at Teignmouth in September of 1997 but the day before I was due to leave, disaster struck. My mother was rushed into hospital seriously ill. This left me not knowing whether I ought to take my holiday or cancel it altogether. If I cancelled it at the last moment, I would still have to pay the full amount. I hurriedly talked it over with Joan and Les, my sister and brother-in-law. They advised me to take the holiday and promised to keep in touch every day to let me know how things were progressing at the hospital. With very real guilt feelings I agreed and promised that I would get on the next train back if things went seriously wrong.

In the circumstances, I could not be of much help. Mother was delirious for most of the time I was away. By the time I got back she had recovered sufficiently to recognise me but I don't think she realised that I had been away at all.

I did not enjoy that holiday very much because I was waiting for what I thought would be the inevitable telephone call summoning me back home. Merry, on the other hand, made the most of her holiday, bossing all the other dogs about and enjoying the organised dog runs, in spite of having stolen a lady's cakes along the promenade, an incident of course, she had simply forgotten all about.

On the Monday morning after my return home I received a telephone call from the Guide Dog Centre asking if they could visit me and introduce me to a dog they thought might suit me.

Things must have changed at the Training Centre, I thought, because I had never been asked to view a new dog before I even started training.

At the appointed time on Thursday morning, Terry and Jane turned up with Fable. This was the second surprise. Strictly speaking I was not a student yet but I was assured that students and instructors now addressed each other by their first names. This was a step in the right direction I thought, as it would mean that the atmosphere would be more relaxed. I smiled as I considered what would happen if one of the dogs was named after any of the staff and had to be corrected. This was no joke because many of the dogs were named after people.

Terry explained that Jane was part of the dog supply unit and was assisting Terry in training some of the dogs. If I accepted, she would be training me but would be supervised by Terry. I liked them both very much; they were so friendly and understanding. Merry must have wondered what was going on but Terry advised me to leave her on her bed while Fable was in the house. Fable was left in the car for a short time while Terry sat talking to me telling me about her. Then he suggested that Jane should bring Fable in to meet me. As soon as she was allowed, she began to examine the surroundings giving me a quick sniff just to find out who I was. When Terry thought that Fable had settled enough, he suggested that Jane should put the harness on Fable so that we could all take a brief walk. Terry brought up the rear obviously so that he could observe how I walked with the dog. It was nine years since I had trained so I was anxious not to make any mistakes. I did my utmost to use my voice properly and also to give the right hand signals. After such a long time little details were bound to slip out of place. I must admit that I felt a little tense as we progressed. I silently prayed that I would be able to cope with the training now I was that bit older. I need not have worried because Terry smiled as he told me later that the Association was training people in their eighties and even older. When we got home, I accepted but I had to explain that my mother was seriously ill and that if I was needed at home during the training period, I hoped that special arrangements could be made in circumstances which would obviously be beyond my control. Terry was very understanding and assured me that should the worst happen special arrangements could be made. He told me that the class was due to start on the following Friday which gave me exactly a week to prepare, and also come to terms with the fact that it was time for Merry to be handed over to her new owners.

Chris came to collect her with the two little girls on the following Thursday before I was due to set out for Leamington the following day. The parting was very distressing for me but I tried hard not to shed tears in front of the two little girls. As the door closed behind them and I heard the car drive off, I let go and let the tears flow. As I wept, I resolved that this was going to be the last time I would give a dog up who had served me faithfully for the past nine years. Merry was gone, but I would make Fable the last Guide Dog I would have. I had faced retirement four times already and found it so stressful I did not think I could find the courage again. However long Fable stayed with me, I determined that when she grew too old to work, I would keep her with me and not have another Guide Dog.

The next day I was off to the Training Centre where I met

my class companions already gathered. This class was to be a busy one. Seven of us started on the Friday and were joined by four more students on the following Monday. We were told that during the three weeks training period at the Centre, the class numbers would rise and fall. This was because some people would only need assessments, or they could only spare a certain amount of time away from work. In other cases, elderly people were being trained at home in their own areas and then being brought into the Centre to do obstacle course training. The intake rose to sixteen. It must have been one of the biggest classes ever run as the centre was full to capacity. This in itself was another thing that was changing. More and more people were coming forward for training and the Association still had to keep up with replacements.

Nothing had changed where the training was concerned. Everything was exactly the same. I know that some people find the three weeks we are required to spend away from home particularly boring especially if they are busy people and have to take the time off work. On the other hand, many find the training period a bit of a holiday, especially if they live alone. The three weeks spent at the centre with other people to talk to probably cheers them up no end. I always made sure I took plenty of reading material with me, or something to do, as I waited for my turn to go out training.

As we grew to know each other, most of the students would gather in the bar in the evenings when the talk would usually centre around Guide Dogs. We would swap stories about our experiences, or laugh about some of the things the general public believed about Guide Dogs. I suppose we should not blame the ordinary man in the street for thinking our dogs can read the numbers on buses, or tell the time. It must look as though they can at times. They can learn words so quickly that sometimes you have to trick them by spelling things out. Once you have been somewhere for the first time and given it a name, you never have to worry about going back again because the dog will find it for you.

I remember hearing about a man whose dog liked a drink of water before going for a free run. As soon as he entered the park he would tell his dog to find the bucket. His dog would then take him across a wide expanse of grass to where a water tap was situated in the middle of the park. I do not believe he could have found the tap on his own.

Much to the embarrassment of some owners, it has been known for some dogs to get it wrong, especially if they were trained by a member of the opposite sex to the present owner. Instead of taking the owner to the Gents or Ladies as the case may be, the owner finished up very much inconvenienced, if you see what I mean. This is quite a common occurrence and only spoken of among Guide Dog owners.

We chuckled over the story of a lady who was taken to the barbers instead of the hairdressers. Presumably, that dog had been trained by a man.

We laughed at the story of the man who thought he could trick his dog. Every Sunday he would put on his best suit to go to church. One day, he put his best suit on to go to work expecting his dog to take him to church. Instead, his dog took him to work as usual. I imagine that dog must have said to himself: "Six days shall ye labour but on the seventh, I will take you to church". Nobody has been able to explain how that dog knew it was an ordinary working day and not Sunday. The man obviously gave the game away quite unconsciously.

Some dogs get some really funny ideas. Someone told us about the organist who always lit his pipe as he left the church so that he could have a smoke on the way home. Unless he took his pipe out of his pocket and lit it, his dog would not budge. I suppose dogs like things to be done in the right order so look out those owners who forget and get it wrong.

There were roars of laughter when I told my companions about the time Biddy stole a baby's bottle out of a pram as we passed a shop. I did not realise that she had anything in her mouth until the distraught mother caught up with me just before I reached my mother-in-law's garden gate. "Excuse me," she yelled, "can I have my baby's bottle?" I stopped dead.

"I haven't got your baby's bottle," I said in a bewildered tone. "You may not have it," she replied breathlessly, "but your dog has it in its mouth. You have been going so fast I could not catch you. I saw you pass the shop and I saw the dog take the bottle, but I could not catch you up!", the poor girl said almost in tears. I looked in Biddy's mouth and found the bottle. Apologising, and feeling a complete fool, I handed it back.

That wasn't so bad as the time Biddy tried to retrieve me from swimming in the sea. We had taken the boys down to the beach one day, and I asked my husband who didn't like swimming to hold Biddy on the lead while I went in with the boys. There was another couple already bathing and they also had an airbed.

All was well until one of the boys shouted that Biddy was swimming towards us. When she came up to me she tried to get hold of me by grabbing any part of me she could find. The young couple called over to me telling me to make for the airbed. Unfortunately, Biddy came after me and tried climbing on the bed. All she succeeded in doing was puncturing the airbed with her claws and scratching my back badly as we sank to the bottom. Fortunately, we were not in deep water so no harm was done. Everyone was in stitches over that one.

One story that was doing the rounds was about a man whose dog always put its paws up on the counter when his owner was making a purchase. He would watch carefully as the change was handed over. He used to tease any customers standing nearby that the dog was making sure he got the right change. This story was highly suspect because no self respecting Guide Dog owner would allow such bad behaviour from a Guide Dog, but there are those among the public who attribute Guide Dogs in particular with more intelligence than they actually have. They really believe these stories. It would be difficult to convince them that what the dog was really doing was checking to see whether the man had anything edible in his hand.

We had a jolly good laugh at the story about the lady who was asked to draw the winning raffle ticket. She pulled the ticket out and held it up for someone to announce the winning number but her Guide Dog grabbed it and ate it. We all fell about laughing at that one.

It is quite easy to get the wrong dog if two dogs are running together. On this occasion, two friends were giving their dogs a run but Harry was on his way to the vet to keep an appointment. His dog was due for a booster injection and in due course he turned up at the surgery in plenty of time. He had barely got into the surgery when the door burst open just as the vet was about to deliver the injection. "You've got the wrong dog.", cried his friend. Well, the vet had a good laugh even though the owners involved felt thoroughly embarrassed. That particular story made the local paper and also the Sun newspaper. Imagine Harry's surprise when he got a phone call from a relative telling him he had made the front page of The Sun.

These gatherings helped us to keep our minds off thoughts from our old dogs that we had recently left behind. I found that my thoughts were constantly straying and wondering how Merry was, hoping that she had settled down in her new home. It was so difficult to transfer my affection to a new dog immediately, nine years had passed since I trained previously and whilst I now had a young dog full of the joys of spring, I was not quite so energetic as I had once been. It was very difficult not to compare the old experienced dog with the newcomer. I am sure it was the same for most of us and we were just putting a brave face on things as we gathered in the evenings to laugh over the various funny, or embarrassing situations our dogs had landed us in.

When Terry first brought Fable out to meet me, I went to great lengths to explain Merry's fear of fireworks, etc. He was quick to assure me that Fable had no fears of that kind. I took his word for it at that stage but Guy Fawkes night fell during the training period giving me the opportunity to observe for myself how Fable reacted.

We did what is known as a night walk as part of the training programme. This helps the dogs to experience working in the dark. The night chosen for our night walk happened to be Guy Fawkes night. I walked all the way down Warwick Road with fireworks banging, rocketing and whizzing into the air all about me. Fable took it all in her stride, in fact, when I got back to the centre and put her in the run she ran down to the bottom fence to get a better view. I must say, I was heartily relieved to know that I would no longer have any further trouble in that direction.

Before we left Leamington, several members of the class took the opportunity to visit Tollgate House where the breeding and puppy walking schemes are carried out. Tollgate House is the largest dog breeding centre in the world. It is situated just outside Leamington at Bishops Tachbrook where it stands in idyllic grounds. Before the Association opened Tollgate, breeding was still on a relatively small scale. Under the guidance of Derek Freeman, of Blue Peter fame, who was then the breeding and puppy walking manager, the centre's role in the work of the Association developed rapidly. The new facilities, including the purpose-built kennels and an expert staff, made it possible to expand the breeding programme. The breeding of Guide Dogs is highly specialised since it aims to develop certain characteristics that have nothing to do with the looks of the dog for showing purposes. It was the emphasis of breeding for temperament that led to crossbred Labradors and Golden Retrievers being so favoured and therefore resulted in producing so many successful Guide Dogs. Of course, Labradors and Golden Retrievers, plus German Shepherds and other suitable breeds are still used respectively, but the majority of the Association's dogs are crossed Labradors and Golden Retrievers these days. The Association no longer has to rely on donated dogs that often turned out to be unsuitable, or sick. Maybe their owners could no longer look after them for any number of reasons. It no longer has to buy dogs in, largely because of the success of the breeding and puppy-walking schemes. The Association has now got a ready supply of specially bred dogs of their own. All puppies born at Tollgate

are potential Guide Dogs. Those who don't make the grade are used as brood bitches and stud dogs. As soon as the pups are old enough, they are sent out to puppy walkers who have the job of socialising the pup and taking it into situations it might meet as a Guide Dog. They do this on a voluntary basis rearing them until they are about ten to twelve months old. I am sure I speak for all fellow Guide Dog owners when I say we are truly grateful to this dedicated band of dog lovers who work so hard on our behalf.

We were all fascinated with the little pups we saw. There were two litters ready to go out to puppy walkers the next day. A litter of Labradors and also one of German Shepherds who made so much noise you would have thought someone was harming them.

The Association keeps a record of all the dogs that are born at Tollgate, and also the parentage so that the best qualities in each dog can be monitored and passed on through the genes to the next generation. We soon turned our attention to the record book anxious to learn the names of the dogs that had sired our dogs, and the name of the dam. I was fortunate on that day as Fable's father happened to be at Tollgate when we visited. He was a big Labrador called Otto and very friendly with it. I did not have the pleasure of meeting Fable's mother who was the brood bitch and called Emma. Of course, we were not allowed to take our dogs with us because the young pups would have become too excited, and because of the danger of unwanted disease creeping into kennels. I think I speak for all of us when I say that I spent a very happy hour at Tollgate House before returning to the Leamington training centre.

As soon as I returned home I rang Chris who assured me that Merry was just fine. She had settled down and was enjoying plenty of free runs and walks with the girls. I was also relieved to hear that the family had got through Guy Fawkes night without incident. Chris reported that luckily, they had not been bothered by many fireworks going off in their area.

Before I left the Centre, I had been given the name and address of Fable's puppy walker. One of the first things I did on arriving home was to sit down and write to Jackie and her family. I wanted her to know that Fable had qualified, and to thank her for all the care she had given her during the time she had her. I hope she got the photograph of Fable and I together in time for Christmas.

My mother was still in hospital when I arrived home with Fable. When Terry came out on his first aftercare visit in December, he taught Fable and I the route from the bus stop down to the hospital ward. When he was satisfied that I knew the way, he left with instructions to try it on my own that afternoon. Feeling confident I set out. On reaching my goal I congratulated myself on my success, but my satisfaction in finding the way was short lived. I never had to do that short walk again because my mother died the next day, just a week before Christmas.

Fable was soon winning hearts just as the other dogs had done over the years. She settled down surprisingly quickly. In no time life began to return to normal and I was going about my daily life much as I had with Merry. She was quick to learn and showed no fear of hot air balloons, a fact that pleased me enormously. It meant that I would no longer be restricted when I wanted to go out. I looked forward to the summer and soon began to plan for my annual holiday down in Teignmouth. I hoped it would be more successful than the last holiday when I had been so worried about my mother. I put those sad thoughts behind me and prepared to meet old friends once again.

Unfortunately, things went badly wrong right at the start of my holiday. Not to put too fine a point on it, I got out of bed the following morning having just arrived the day before, and fell over Fable who was lying by the bed. The fall resulted in a broken wrist and I spent Bank Holiday Sunday in casualty at Torbay Hospital being plastered.

I cannot speak highly enough of the staff at Teignmouth who did everything possible to help me, and also to look after Fable. It was impossible for me to walk with Fable on harness, so the kennel girls took her for walks. She was also taken on the organised dog runs where all the dogs are allowed to enjoy themselves running free. I think she got the holiday, but my holiday was slightly disappointing. I consoled myself with the thought that at least one of us had a good time, and that I would have better luck when I came back next year. On my return everything went well. Fable got the doggy runs, and I had a successful holiday. I remembered Terry's words as my friend and I left Teignmouth to return home. As we left the hotel, it started to thunder. We sat on Teignmouth station undercover while the most horrendous storm burst over our heads. Terry had told me that Fable was bomb proof. I certainly found out that day just how bomb proof she was. Now I had no worries. My mind was finally made easy. It had now been proven that Fable had no fears of thunder, fireworks or hot air balloons. I silently thanked my good fortune because I cannot imagine how I would have coped with Merry in such a situation.

When I got home I rang the centre telling them about my accident and the damage to my wrist. They agreed that Fable should go back until my wrist had healed enough for me to handle her again. It was to be two months before she was returned to me. In the meantime, I had to learn to use the long cane. I had vivid memories of using a white stick when I was young but being without a Guide Dog left me with little option if I was to maintain any semblance of independence. Where one would creep along a wall with a white stick, the technique of using a long cane was to make an arc movement in front of you thus locating any obstacle that may lie ahead. The technique did not present a problem, but having the confidence to go out alone using a long cane instead of the ease of a Guide Dog, certainly took a toll on my nervous system. I thought I would never find the courage, but by the time Fable was returned to me, I had mastered the art, although I did not enjoy it.

It was amazing how many people would stop me in the street and ask me where my dog was. Whenever I went into a shop I used regularly, there would be the inevitable questions. How was Fable? Did I think she was missing me? How long would I have to have the plaster on? Why could Fable not stay with me? I fielded the questions as best I could convincing all the well wishers that Fable was fine. I noted with a sense of irony that all those good people who asked after Fable, omitted to ask how I was managing. Ah well, I thought, at least they were interested enough to ask about the dog, never mind about my wrist.

Shortly after Fable came back I was off again to spend a fortnight in Spain with my sister who had recently lost her husband. I had arranged with Leamington for Fable to be looked after by a puppy walker who lived in Aylesbury. This was ideal as it meant that I would not have to send her back to

Leamington again so soon after her return.

Jean and Bob were a very pleasant couple. They were walking a puppy called William and they also had a pet Cairn called Freddie. This was excellent for Fable who would have canine company while I was away. When I returned, all was well. Jean told me that they had got on splendidly together and they had all had a wonderful time playing with each other. She called Freddie the outrider because he liked to run alongside Fable and William and keep up with the big guys.

Fable spent a further two weeks with Jean and Bob this year. William had gone back to the centre for training and they now had a new pup called Wilky. Jean laughed as she told me the story of how she had taken Fable to church in order to do the flowers. All her friends congratulated her on how well they thought she was doing with Wilky's training. They said how good they thought he was to sit so quietly while she was busy. She told them to take a good look and they would see that it was not Wilky but another trained Guide Dog she was looking after.

The same kind of incident would often happen when Jean and Bob were running the dogs. Friends would often remark how big Wilkie had suddenly grown. "Look again," Jean would say, "that is a different dog altogether. This one is a trained Guide Dog." Bob chuckled as he told me how the dogs used to play with the toys together and how clever Fable was at getting the one she really wanted. Wilkie would sit on the toys in his bed. Fable would grab any one she could get hold of and then wave it around in front of Wilkie to entice Wilkie to take it. As soon as he moved she was in like a shot. Grabbing the toy she really wanted, she was off at a rate of knots.

I have now been a Guide Dog owner for forty years and as I look back I remember all the dogs and their owners that I met each time I went through the training process when my old dog came to the end of its working life. Every one of my dogs has enabled me to live a full and active life. They have each given me independence, loyalty and companionship over the years. I have been able to go out when I wished and not had to wait for someone to come along and take me. I have had the freedom of being able to walk through heavy traffic without worrying. I have had the satisfaction of being able to find shops, or a particular house without stopping the first person who comes by to ask for assistance. A Guide Dog does all these things for the owner and much more besides.

I have travelled extensively throughout the country, given talks and met many interesting people who always asked about my Guide Dog. I have coped with a family and brought up four children, and done many other things as well. I am not an exception however, I am just an ordinary person. Others have achieved much more than myself, but I doubt whether I would have been able to do half as much over the years, if I had not had the help of my dogs.

Not all blind people share my enthusiasm for dogs. After all, we are all individuals and if a person does not like animals or feels the responsibility of caring for a dog would be too much, there is certainly no point in having one. A strong bond has to be built up between the dog and owner. That is why it is necessary for us to attend a training centre each time we need a new dog.

Today, the white harness of a Guide Dog is a well-known sight in every large town and city in Britain. The Association

FABLE

has now been established in this country for seventy years. It started as a very small organisation in 1931 when just four men were successfully trained.

Since then, the Association has grown and now has seven training centres, the first being opened in Leamington in 1939 then Exeter in 1951, followed by Bolton and then Forfar. Another centre opened at Wokingham in 1977, then came Middlesborough in 1983. A further centre to serve London opened in Redbridge in 1985, and also a further centre at Lark Hill, Scotland in 1990. There are three satellite centres to take up the slack serving Belfast, Cardiff and Maidstone.

To date, there are a total of 4750 units currently working in the U.K. The Guide Dogs for the Blind Association is one of the biggest charities in the country and it has given many blind people independence. I have every confidence that it will continue to do so in the coming century.

THE END